Everybody's Birthday Book

Birthdays are always exciting, and if you can look up your birthdate and see which famous people were born then or what important event occurred, it makes them even more fun. George and Cornelia Kay list interesting events day by day, and include lots of fascinating facts and folklore about the changing year. Every month has a page where you can fill in the birthdays of your friends and relatives, to help you remember them, and there is even a chapter on tricks and stunts so you can surprise people by finding out their age and on which day of the week they were born.

Mr and Mrs Kay have written a number of books for children, including *The Beaver Book of Games*, also published by Hamlyn.

Everybody's Birthday Book

George and Cornelia Kay

Illustrated by Annie Bennett
and Peter Dennis

Beaver Books

First published in 1977 by
The Hamlyn Publishing Group Limited
London · New York · Sydney · Toronto
Astronaut House, Feltham, Middlesex, England

© Copyright Text George and Cornelia Kay 1977
© Copyright Illustrations
The Hamlyn Publishing Group Limited 1977
ISBN 0 600 31424 3

Printed in England by Cox & Wyman Limited
London, Reading and Fakenham
Set in Monotype Bembo

The illustration by E. H. Shepard, reproduced on
page 27 by kind permission of Curtis Brown Limited
and the Estate of E. H. Shepard, is copyright under
the Berne Convention.

The illustration on page 71 by William Heath
Robinson is taken from *Absurdities,* and reproduced
by kind permission of Gerald Duckworth and
Company Limited.

Contents

The Days

When we talk about a day's date we usually mean a period of both day and night lasting for twenty-four hours, from one midnight to the next. Actually astronomers and space scientists have to bear in mind that the day is not exactly twenty-four hours long. If the time is worked out by reference to a star the time is a few seconds shorter than twenty-four hours; if it is checked by the sun it is a few seconds longer. So that we don't all have to alter clocks and watches every day to meet this difference, the day's length is worked out from an imaginary sun. The position of the real sun and the imaginary sun coincides only on four days a year – around April 15, June 15, August 31, and December 24.

In times gone by many people did not consider that the new day began at midnight. Some preferred midday (when the sun was at its zenith) and many others chose the variable time when dawn came.

Our Saxon ancestors in Britain and many parts of Europe chose summertime dawn as the start of a new day and then divided the rest of the day and night into three-hour periods. The Saxon language is difficult for us to pronounce, but you can see in some of the names for these periods how we use words which are quite similar to theirs. Here are the names the Saxons used:

Morgan (4.30 a.m.–7.30 a.m.), Dael-mael (7.30 a.m.–10.30 a.m.),
Middaeg (10.30 a.m.–1.30 p.m.), Ofanverthrdager (1.30 p.m.–4.30 p.m.),

Midaften (4.30 p.m.–7.30 p.m.), Ondverthnot (7.30 p.m.–10.30 p.m.), Midniht (10.30 p.m.–1.30 a.m.), Fanverthnot (1.30 a.m.–4.30 a.m.).

Of course the Saxons had no clocks, so the times of the periods were not as exact as suggested here, but if they could describe roughly a three-hour period this was good enough for most of their activities: 'It rained all through Dael-mael'; 'I can get to the market before Middaeg'; 'The Chief will go hunting during midniht'.

For centuries people did not worry overmuch about the exact time of the day. In the fourteenth century the Black Prince was probably quite content to give orders to his troops simply by saying they would march at morningtide, noontide, or eventide. There were a few clocks by then, but ordinary soldiers would not have been able to tell the time even if they saw one of these marvels.

It was more important for our ancestors to have names for days. The Romans had the idea of naming them after the heavenly bodies in the sky, taking them in the order of the distance they believed they were from the earth: Sun, Moon, Mars, Mercury, Jupiter, Venus, Saturn.

As the Roman Empire covered all of Europe and parts of Africa and Asia the conquered peoples gradually adopted this bright idea of naming the days, sometimes keeping the Roman names but mostly changing them to honour their own gods.

Sunday in Old England was Sunnandaeg, meaning day of the Sun, the most powerful god.

Monday was Monandaeg, the day of the Moon, goddess of hunting.

Tuesday was Tyrdaeg, the day of Tyr, son of Odin and a god of war.

Wednesday was Wodnesdaeg, the day of Woden, usually known as Odin, the god of wisdom and bravery.

Thursday was Thordaeg, the day of Thor, the god of thunder.

Friday was Frigedaeg, the day of Fregga, wife of Odin and goddess of love.

Saturday was Saeternesdaeg, the day of the Roman god Saturn, father of many children.

As every day had its own god or goddess our ancestors believed that good fortune would come by starting any activity related to that divinity on that day. Thus it was best to go hunting during the night of a Monday when the moon was full or to marry on Friday. And the day of one's birth controlled the occupation it would be best to follow in adult life. So a Tuesday baby was expected to become a great warrior, and one born on a Wednesday would become a wise chieftain or priest.

We still have rhymes supposed to prophesy the future life according to the day on which we were born. Here are two versions: the first has probably been recited since Elizabeth I ruled England, the second was written down nearly two hundred years ago.

> Born on Monday, fair of face.
> Born on Tuesday, full of grace.
> Born on Wednesday, sour and sad.
> Born on Thursday, merry and glad.
> Born on Friday, worthily given.
> Born on Saturday, work hard for your living.
> Born on Sunday, you will never know want.

> Monday's child is fair of face.
> Tuesday's child is full of grace.
> Wednesday's child is full of woe.
> Thursday's child has far to go.
> Friday's child is loving and giving.
> Saturday's child works hard for his living.
> But the child who is born on the Sabbath day
> Is lucky and happy and good and gay.

If you want to be amused by the meaning of something you cannot control on a particular day here is a rhyme recited to children for hundreds of years whenever they sneezed.

> Sneeze on a Monday, you sneeze for danger.
> Sneeze on a Tuesday, you'll meet a stranger.
> Sneeze on a Wednesday, you'll be getting a letter.
> Sneeze on a Thursday, you'll get something better.
> Sneeze on a Friday, you sneeze for sorrow.
> Sneeze on a Saturday, see your best friend tomorrow.
> Sneeze on a Sunday, your safety seek
> The Devil will chase you the whole of the week.

The Week

A week of seven days was adopted by the Israelites when their leader Moses handed them God's ten commandments, which included the order to work for six days and rest on the seventh. That was at least 3200 years ago, so it is a very ancient time measurement, and, of course, it has spread through Christianity to every corner of the earth.

But there were not always seven days in a week. When Moses lived as a little boy in Ancient Egypt the week he knew was ten days long. The Greeks copied this idea, but the Romans mostly preferred a week of eight working days followed by a rest day. They did not change to the seven-day week till almost the end of the Empire.

Many smaller nations devised a week which was most suitable for them, usually based on market days. In a scattered community people did not need to buy and sell more frequently than every ten days, so this became the length of their week. Others might have found it profitable to hold markets every four days, and in many primitive countries the four-day week was usual.

Often, in more recent times, nations have tried to find a better length for the week. After the French Revolution there was a ten-day week in the Republic. Napoleon cancelled it when he became Emperor. Russia ordered her people to follow a five-day week in 1929; this proved too short and three years later it became a six-day week. Finally, in 1940, Russia adopted the

universal seven days followed by the rest of the world.

Everyone will probably agree that seven days are the ideal, for human beings need to have a rhythm in their activities, with a special day for rest, recreation and devotion to religion. Seven days seem best. People can work hard for six days so long as they have a break for a day before starting all over again, while anything longer brings exhaustion and bad work. But in many ways we now have a shorter week, with two extra days which do not count. We talk about the five-day working week, which most people now enjoy, with two days to do whatever they want at the end of one week and the start of the next.

The Months

Thirty days hath September,
April, June, and November.
All the rest have thirty-one
Excepting February alone,
Which has but twenty-eight days clear,
And twenty-nine each leap year.

Without this very old rhyme it would be difficult for us to remember how many days there are in each month. All sorts of ideas have been offered to give us months which are all the same length, but none of them fits nicely into the 365 days of the year like the twelve months of different lengths which we now have.

The difficulty was realised as soon as people needed to divide the year into periods. The Sumerians, who lived on the banks of the rivers Tigris and Euphrates 5000 years ago, seem to have had twelve months, each of thirty days, which left five days at the end of the year which were not in any month.

The Babylonians tried to improve this system by having months of thirty days alternating with months of twenty-nine days. Every three years or so they simply added an extra month of thirty days to correct the steadily increasing error. The Babylonians were very clever astronomers, and they had discovered by about 500 B.C. that the moon – which they used as the time-table for the length of a month – made exactly 235 circuits of the earth in nineteen years. To make their calendar match the moon's circuits they then added an extra month for seven out of every nineteen years, and so got the total of 235 months exactly right.

Their neighbours, the Egyptians, did not think much of this system. Their priests worked out that the year was almost exactly 365 days long, so they devised names for twelve months of thirty days each. That, as usual, left five days unaccounted for, and the Pharaohs passed a law most of us would like today. Five days were set aside in midsummer for feasting and celebrations.

At this time the Israelites had their own calendar, and the Bible stories give a few of the names for their months. Abib was the first month of their year, Zif the second. The other months which are mentioned are Ethanim and Bul, the seventh and eighth months.

The ancient Greeks at first did not bother much about dividing the year into months, but when they decided some sort of division would be useful the local folk invented their own, so that a traveller going from one city to another would find a bewildering variety of names and periods. Months which were supposed to occur at sowing time, midsummer, harvesting and mid-winter were soon hopelessly inaccurate. But this problem was easily solved – simply by repeating a month now and then.

When the Romans adopted the idea of having months they first named ten periods for the year. This was, of course, very inaccurate and they soon changed to a twelve-month year. The Romans were a very superstitious people and considered even numbers unlucky, so instead of having some months with thirty days they had a month of twenty-nine days followed by one of thirty-one days. These totalled 360 days for the year, which were more than five days too few, and once again a monthly calendar got hopelessly out of tune with Nature.

When Julius Caesar was ruling the Roman Empire he put things right. In 46 B.C. he decreed that this was to be a very unusual year – 445 days long, with twenty-three days added to

February and sixty-seven to November.

The Romans gave the months names which we still use. Some were named in honour of their gods or natural events – January for Janus, February for Februa, March for Mars, (which was the first month of their year), Aprilis (the opening of plant buds) for April, May for Maia, mother of Mercury, and June for Juno. Julius Caesar gave his name to July, and another Roman Emperor, Caesar Augustus, to August. After that they seem to have run out of ideas and just used the number for the month – September, October, November, and December, which were the seventh, eighth, ninth and tenth months for their year, as it began in March.

So, with a few small changes, the months devised by the Caesars of ancient Rome are still in use today.

Although the exact period of a month obviously has no effect on the weather most of us like to think that each new month brings a marked change in the climate – 'Oh to be be in England now that April's there,' as the poet Browning wrote, while a hot day or two in midsummer makes everyone talk about 'flaming June'.

An eighteenth-century poet named George Ellis wrote a poem called *The Twelve Months* in which he summed up the weather for each month from January to December thus:

> Snowy Flowy Blowy
> Showery Flowery Bowery
> Hoppy Croppy Droppy
> Breezy Sneezy Freezy

The Year

Exactly how long will this year be? It's easy to say that it is the time the earth takes to revolve round the sun or to mention 365 days. Neither is really the precise answer. Space scientists and astronomers have to make special observations, but for most folk it is enough to say that the year is 365 days plus 5 hours 28 minutes and 46 seconds long.

Those extra hours, minutes and seconds mean that every year our calendar gets a little behind the correct time, and this is put right with an extra day for Leap Year every fourth year, when the date can be divided by four, unless that year is the last of the century and cannot be divided by 400. Thus 1980 and 1984, and every fourth year after them, will be Leap Years, and so will the year 2000. But 1900 was not a Leap Year because it cannot be exactly divided by 400.

In whatever year you are reading this you may be sure that the number is wrong. The birth of Jesus Christ, from which the years of our era are counted, was certainly not in Anno Domini 1, but at least four years earlier, so to name this year correctly you should add four to the number on a calendar.

The reason this mistake occurred is quite simple. Nearly 1400 years ago a monk named Dionysius Exiguus invented our present system of dating historical events either B.C. or A.D. He made a silly mistake in his arithmetic and got the year A.D. 1 in the wrong place. No one noticed the error for a thousand years. To have changed all the historical records would have caused enormous trouble, so the mistake has remained uncorrected.

Many people still retain other numbers for their years. In the Jewish calendar what is 1978 to most people is 5738 and already four months old on January 1. For Muslim people the year beginning on December 2, 1978 is 1399, and in parts of India 1978 is 2035 and in other areas of that country 1900. And all over the world men who are Freemasons conduct their formal business in both the conventional calendar and also their own – Anno Domini 1978 and Anno Lucis 5978.

Most of us know the joke about the man who said he found some ancient coins dated 55 B.C. and managed to sell them to someone who did not appreciate immediately that they must be forgeries! But have you ever paused to think how people numbered the year before our present system was invented?

Among ancient peoples the usual practice was to number them according to the years the king had reigned, starting at year 1 again when a new king came to the throne. The Greeks were among the first to choose an original date and continued it year after year. They chose their great event of the Olympic Games which took place – as now – every four years, and began with the Games held in 776 B.C.

The Romans numbered their years from an event a little later than that of the Greeks – 753 B.C., when they believed the twins Romulus and Remus founded the city of Rome.

The Roman system was used for hundreds of years all over the known world. Apart from the fact that it was a non-Christian method of numbering a year, the duration as devised by Julius Caesar was inaccurate, and gradually countries adopted the B.C.–A.D. system, though not altering the number of days in the year.

By the sixteenth century the calendar was so badly out of joint with the season that in 1582 Pope Gregory ordered that October 5 should be re-numbered October 15. All the Catholic nations of Europe duly changed their calendars, but in Britain and other Protestant countries the old system was retained. In

Britain the change was not made until 1752. Crowds angrily protested, gathering outside the king's palace and the Houses of Parliament, yelling 'give us back our eleven days' in the belief that they were being deprived of eleven days of their lives.

At the same time New Year's Day became January 1. Previously it had been March 25 though many people insisted on regarding Christmas Day as the first day of the new year. We still recall that March start to the year, calling March 25 Lady Day, with many legal and financial affairs ending and starting afresh on or close to that day.

China had its own calendar for at least 3000 years, with the year based on the Pole Star and the planet Jupiter, the Chinese New Year occurring either in late January or early February. In 1911 the government decided to adopt our calendar, so officially the Chinese New Year's Day is January 1. But almost all Chinese people still celebrate it in the old way. Children receive presents and workers have a holiday. Firecrackers are let off in the streets and Dragon and Lion dancers roam through the villages and towns. Friends and strangers alike are greeted with '*kung lei fat choy*' – 'happy new year' in Chinese.

Every year, apart from being numbered in the European style, is given the name of a creature – animal, fish or reptile – chosen by astrologers. 1977 was the year of the snake, bringing luck to lovers.

The Stars
on your Birthday

Thousands of years ago, when the people of Babylon were mostly wandering nomads, moving with their flocks of sheep and goats from place to place, they had good opportunities to study the glittering stars in the clear night skies of Arabia. They noticed that there was a wide belt extending across the heavens which contained the visible planets as well as the sun and the moon, and many stars twinkling in groups. They divided the belt into twelve sections, each section as a division of the year, marked by the entry of the sun as it seemed to move from east to west into a group of stars.

You can see the Zodiac belt for yourself on some cloudless and moonless nights as a faint haze of light just above the western horizon after sunset or the eastern horizon before dawn. The best times for observation are evenings in March or early mornings in September, and the best place is the countryside, because the glare of lights in the sky above towns usually spoils the milky light of the Zodiac belt.

The Babylonians gave each division of the Zodiac a name and a sign. In the British Museum in London is a Babylonian stone with these signs of the Zodiac. It was carved about 1180 B.C., which shows how old are those signs you see in horoscope features in magazines and newspapers.

For our remote ancestors who believed all the heavenly bodies revolved round a stationary earth, the movements of the stars, sun and moon seemed to have divine significance, and must affect the future life of a person according to the sign under which he or she was born. Thus they believed that one period forecast a future of wealth, another favoured artistic work, a third skill in hunting, and so on. Gradually this idea of a strange influence coming from the sky gave rise to the idea that every year and every day of a person's life was affected by the stars, and astrologers worked out the planets' positions, claiming to know what they signified for each person who was prepared to pay for the specialised advice they could offer.

No modern astronomer believes that astrology is a real science, and for most of us reading our horoscope prediction is just an amusement, mainly interesting to see how right or wrong it was by the end of the day.

Due to a slight change in the angle of the earth's axis to its path round the sun which occurs year after year the signs of the Zodiac as originally worked out are now incorrect. The period the ancient astrologers would have called Aries is now Pisces, so even if we are tempted to believe the wise men of old, today's positions of the stars do not have the influences originally claimed.

But just for fun you may like to know what your birth sign is supposed to signify. Incidentally, the precise beginning and end of each period change by a day or two periodically, as you will see from the 'stars' feature in a newspaper.

ARIES, the Ram (March 21–April 19), rules the mind. Its subjects are enterprising and impatient. They make good explorers, soldiers and architects.

TAURUS, the Bull (April 20–May 20), rules the neck and throat. Taureans are kind and determined. They may become great singers or succeed in any creative work.

GEMINI, the Twins (May 21–June 21), rule the limbs and lungs. Their subjects are rather fickle and excitable, but energetic and helpful to others. They make good writers and artists.

CANCER, the Crab (June 22–July 22), rules the stomach. Its persuasive and rather moody subjects often become salesmen or teachers.

LEO, the Lion (July 23–August 22), rules the heart. Proud, generous, and full of energy, Leos are successful in politics and entertainment.

VIRGO, the Virgin (August 23–September 22), rules the digestion. Subjects are methodical and eager to serve others, but liable to quarrel. They excel in craft work and nursing.

LIBRA, the Scales (September 23–October 23), rules the kidneys. Librans tend to be lazy, but are just in their treatment of others. They may become famous statesmen or directors of successful businesses.

SCORPIO, the Scorpion (October 24–November 21), rules love and friendship. These highly emotional subjects may become good doctors or take up a religious life.

SAGITTARIUS, the Archer (November 22–December 21), rules the legs. These strong and athletic people are destined to travel or to take up hard physical work.

CAPRICORN, the Goat (December 22–January 19), rules the knees. People born at this time of year are shy but ambitious.

They are good at organising work and controlling others.

AQUARIUS, the Water Carrier (January 20–February 18), rules the ankles. Aquarians are rather careless and dislike strict rules, but they are considerate of others and get on in life by relying on hunches. They may become scientists and thinkers.

PISCES, the Fish (February 19–March 20), rules the feet. These subjects are gentle, and sacrifice themselves for the benefit of others. They are successful as actors and in any kind of welfare work.

Each Zodiac sign has its lucky emblem in the form of a jewel and a colour. They are:

ARIES:	Aquamarine. Sea green.
TAURUS:	Diamond. Clear.
GEMINI:	Emerald. Mid-green.
CANCER:	Pearl. Cream-white.
LEO:	Ruby. Red.
VIRGO:	Peridot. Green.
LIBRA:	Sapphire. Blue.
SCORPIO:	Opal. Multi-coloured.
SAGITTARIUS:	Topaz. Yellow.
CAPRICORN:	Turquoise. Blue-green.
AQUARIUS:	Garnet. Reddish-brown.
PISCES:	Amethyst. Purple.

January

The Happy New Year month is a zestful time, bringing renewed hope for better days ahead, with proof of a fresh start with daylight increasing, at first by a minute and by the end of the month by four minutes every day.

Of course it is also the coldest month (and south of the equator the hottest) though wild gorse and jasmine both put out the very first flowers of spring. And by mid-month there are some snowdrops in bloom even if they have to poke through frosty ground. There is a story that when Adam and Eve left the Garden of Eden an angel changed snowflakes into these tiny white flowers to comfort them and give them hope of happier times.

Scots people have the best January celebration on Hogmanay, which starts on the tick of midnight as the New Year is born. In villages and town communities a man called the First Footer knocks on the door. He brings some bread, salt, and coal, and is invited in without a word being said. He places the bread and salt on a table as symbols of food and friendship, and throws the coal on the fire as a symbol of warmth. As soon as the coal starts to burn the ban of silence is lifted, and the First Footer is given a drink and a small cake. Leaving his hosts to celebrate he goes off to the next house and repeats the ceremony. It is considered very unlucky not to be visited by a First Footer.

Then comes Twelfth Night (January 6), not only the last day for the Christmas and New Year celebrations but a festival welcoming the very first signs of spring. To follow the old ritual the Twelfth Night party should start at midday on January 5, with the Christmas decorations removed and the Christmas tree burned at midnight, followed by singing and eating and drinking till dawn. One article of food should be a large cake in which a single bean has been baked. In the past the guest who found the bean in his piece of cake became King or Queen of the Revels. The festivities had to include all sorts of practical jokes, including making cakes with strange things baked into them instead of a bean. The rhyme about Four and Twenty Blackbirds originally referred to one of these surprise cakes.

Among the early Christians it was believed that Jesus was baptised on January 6, and on that date years later he changed water into wine at the wedding in Cana. As a result people liked to have their babies christened on that day and it was popular for marriages. It was also regarded as the day to bottle wines from the casks in which they had started to ferment the previous autumn.

The weather on January 6 was studied with care as the signs were believed to show what the rest of the year would be like. Strangely, it was hoped the weather would be cold. One old proverb said:

> If January six be summerly gay
> 'Twill be winterly weather till the beginning of May.

January

1. New Year's Day, also known as the Octave of Christmas. It is the anniversary of St Basil the Great, who in the fourth century built an estate in Syria with a hospital, travellers' hostel, houses for the poor, and a staff of doctors and nurses at a time when such help for people was unknown. James Frazer, born on this day

in 1854, was a Scotsman famous for his book *The Golden Bough,* describing the ancient religions and beliefs in magic.

2. The anniversary of the birth of James Wolfe in 1727. His victory when the English troops defeated the French enemy at Quebec ensured that Canada was British.

3. The birthday of two pop stars: Roger Daltrey, vocalist with The Who, and John Paul Jones (real name John Baldwin), Led Zeppelin's pianist.

4. Jacob Grimm was born on this day in 1785. With his brother he recorded the famous fairy tales which they found in old books and learned by talking to peasant people.

5. The birthday of Spain's new king, Juan Carlos I.

6. Twelfth Night, the last day of the Christmas festivities. It is said that on this day the Wise Men reached Bethlehem and made their gifts to the baby Jesus. In many parts of Italy children get presents on this day as well as at Christmas. Joan of Arc, France's national heroine, was born on this day in 1412.

7. The feast day of St Lucian, who was said to have drowned at sea. His body was brought to land for proper burial by a dolphin. The story is one reason why fishermen and sailors never harm these intelligent sea creatures, believing that they will guide ships in distress and may save drowning sailors.

8. Britain's Prime Ministers received a wonderful gift on this day in 1921 when Lord Lee of Fareham gave the country mansion of Chequers in Buckinghamshire as a rural residence for every Prime Minister to enjoy. In 1806 a British expedition occupied the Cape of Good Hope for Britain. It is the birthday of Elvis Presley, king of rock 'n' roll; and of Dennis Wheatley, author of mysteries and thrillers.

9. The birthday of Gracie Fields, famous Lancashire singer and film star.

10. On this day in 1920 the nations of the world made their first effort to ensure world peace when the League of Nations was formed. In 1840 the Penny Post began, with letters collected and delivered for one penny, no matter what the distance they had to be carried. It is the birthday of Rod Stewart, pop singer, guitarist, and composer.

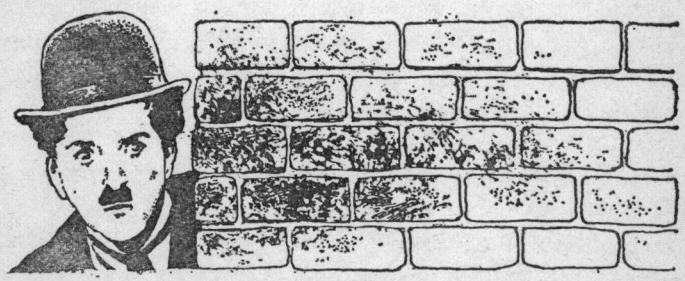

11. On this day in 1914 a young actor completed his first film, *Making a Living*. His name was Charlie Chaplin. This is the feast day of St Theodosius, who lived for 105 years. He devoted his life to helping the old and sick.

12. The feast day of St Benedict Biscop, north-east England's patron saint. He founded monasteries in the seventh century, and started libraries, teaching people to read and write when very few were literate. It is the anniversary of the birthday of John Sargent, American painter of Presidents and other celebrities.

13. The birthday of Ted Willis, who has written hundreds of radio and TV scripts including those for the police series *Dixon of Dock Green*. It is the anniversary of the birth of William Reid Dick in 1879. His sculptures can be seen in many places: the eagle on the RAF memorial on London's Thames Embankment, President Roosevelt in Grosvenor Square, and Lady Godiva in Coventry.

14. The birth dates of two famous Europeans: Albert Schweitzer, a scholar and musician who devoted his long life to caring for the sick in a hospital he built in equatorial Africa; and Pierre Loti, a French novelist whose books are often set for examinations on French literature.

15. The day of the raven. This bird, so often killed because of its attacks on other birds' eggs and its general destructiveness, used to be perfectly safe from man on January 15 in commemoration of St Paul the Hermit, whose feast day this is. Legend tells how ravens daily stole half a loaf from rich men's houses and brought it to Paul in his cave where he lived as a hermit. If the saint had a visitor the ravens brought two pieces of bread.

16. The anniversary of two important events in history: in 1707 England and Scotland signed a treaty bringing to an end the interminable wars between the two countries; and in 1780 Admiral Rodney's defeat of a Spanish fleet in the naval battle of St Vincent saved Gibraltar from having to surrender after a long siege.

17. Many birthdays of famous people of past and present: Benjamin Franklin, American statesman; Anton Chekhov, Russian playwright and story writer; David Lloyd George, Britain's Prime Minister during the later years of the First World War; champion boxer Muhammad Ali.

18. A historic anniversary for Australians, for on this day in 1788 the first ship transporting convicts from Britain dropped anchor in Botany Bay and they built a permanent settlement in an area which is now a suburb of Sydney. And on January 18 in 1912 Captain Robert Scott reached the South Pole with four companions. All unfortunately died on the return journey. One of them who was ill, Lawrence Oates, deliberately crept away so he would not be a hindrance to his friends – the action famous as that 'of a very gallant gentleman'. A happier anniversary is the birth of A. A. Milne who wrote *Winnie the Pooh*.

19. The birthday of Edgar Allan Poe in 1809; he was the author of stories of terror and the originator of the modern detective novel. January 19 is also the birthday of Phil Everly of the Everly Brothers country rock harmony act.

20. The birthday of Telly Savalas, TV's Kojak, and of Roy Plomley, best known for his *Desert Island Discs* radio programme, the longest running record show from the BBC. It was first transmitted in 1942. This is St Agnes's Eve, once said to be a time for dreaming of the future. A girl who wanted to know the name of her future husband would bake a small cake and eat it in bed as she prepared for sleep. In the next hour or so she would see her future husband in a dream.

21. The birthday of Jack Nicklaus, champion golfer. In Spain one family makes this day a special celebration: Señora Olivarez and her four children all have January 21 as their birthday. It is the feast day of St Agnes, the patron saint of little girls; she was a Roman child cruelly put to death when she was only thirteen.

22. Lord Byron, the poet, was born on this day in 1788. He said his hatred of cold weather was the result of being born on a winter's day. In one poem he wrote: 'The English winter ... ending in July, to recommence in August.'

23. This is the feast day of St John the Almsgiver, who more than 1400 years ago founded and paid for hospitals for the birth of babies and gave money to help their mothers. He became the patron saint of the Knights of Malta, whose charitable work gradually developed into the Knights of St John, organising hospital and Red Cross work.

24. The birthdays of two pop stars – Neil Diamond, writer and singer; and Michael Chapman, guitarist, singer and song writer.

25. A great occasion for all Scots folk, when they celebrate the birth of their most famous poet, Robert Burns, with a supper of haggis, readings of his poems and singing his version of *Auld Lang Syne*.

26. Republic Day in India, when the country's independence is celebrated. It is also Australia Day, chosen as the anniversary of the day in 1788 when the first English fleet arrived in Sydney Cove (see January 18) and huts were then built. The ships were

under the command of Captain Arthur Phillips, who became governor of the new colony, which he named New South Wales. It is the birthday of film star Paul Newman.

27. The birthday of Wolfgang Amadeus Mozart in 1756; this artistic genius was composing music and playing the violin in public at the age of five. In the thirty-five years of his life he wrote about 700 works. Another famous man born on this day was C. L. Dodgson, better known as Lewis Carroll, the author of *Alice in Wonderland* and *Alice Through the Looking Glass*.

28. The birthday of Sabine Baring-Gould, who a century ago collected and wrote down hundreds of old English folk songs which would otherwise have been lost for ever. He was also the author of the hymns *Onward Christian Soldiers* and *Now the Day is Over*.

29. The feast day of St Francis de Sales, a Frenchman who became famous for his writings, and was chosen to be the patron saint of authors and journalists. In France it is believed that anyone born on this day is destined for a successful career in literature.

30. Birthday anniversaries of Franklin Roosevelt, most famous of modern US Presidents; Richard Hearne ('Mr Pastry' on TV and in pantomimes); and Vanessa Redgrave, actress daughter of Sir Michael Redgrave.

31. Franz Schubert was born on this day in 1797. He was Viennese and wrote more music than almost any other major composer of his time. It is also the birthday of Christopher Chataway, the man who broke Roger Bannister's 4-minute mile record. This is the feast day of a modern saint, John Bosco, who just over a hundred years ago started hostels and workshops in Turin for boys either very poor or without a family so they could learn a trade. The schools and hostels have since spread all over the world.

January

Birthday Dates	16
1	17
2	18
3	19
4	20
5	21
6	22
7	23
8	24
9	25
10	26
11	27
12	28
13	29
14	30
15	31

February

Candlemas (February 2) is the first of the special days of this month. In ancient Rome it was a feast day in honour of Februa, who was the mother of Mars, the god of war. On that day women walked through the streets carrying lighted candles to place in the goddess' temple beside the river Tiber. When Christianity became the religion of Europe the same processions took place in honour of the Virgin Mary. February 2 is regarded as a very lucky day for the birth of a child or its christening.

Countryfolk also considered it an important day as regards the rest of the year's weather.

> If Candlemas be fair and bright
> Winter will have another flight.
> If Candlemas Day be cloud and rain
> Winter will not come again.

and

> When the wind's in the east on Candlemas Day
> There it will stop till the second of May.

The other great festival day of the month is February 14, St Valentine's Day. Again, this was originally a Roman celebration when young people chose their sweethearts by lottery. In our own era it was believed that the first person seen by any single man or girl on February 14 would one day be the marriage partner, and if girls wanted to know in advance who the lucky man would be they put a bay leaf under their pillow the night before to ensure that they saw him in a dream.

Today millions of Valentine cards are posted without any name of the sender. It was a romantic idea which began about 150 years ago after it became cheap and easy to mail a letter. This custom is almost the only one left of what was once a general holiday and every home displayed a bowl of snowdrops in the window.

February 14 was a significant date. It was the day that badgers were supposed to stir from their winter sleep and look out of their sets. If the sun was shining they went back for more sleep as the winter was by no means over; if there was snow they walked around to wake up properly, certain that the worst of winter would soon pass.

It was also believed that this was the day birds chose their mates. Certainly many birds in early February are convinced spring is on the way. Lapwings pair in February; blackbirds, house sparrows, rooks and tawny owls begin to build their nests, and most birds begin to sing once more.

Plants are also growing in February. Catkins form on hazels and willows. Ivy and nettles put out new leaves, and celandines and daisies mark damp areas with their yellow and white flowers.

February

1. This is Candlemas Eve. For centuries shepherds have regarded today as the most propitious time for lambs to be born, for they will all grow up healthy and strong, and there will be no stillbirths. Many modern farmers still believe that this is true, and in some parts of Wales the day still has its ancient lambing name – Imbole. Stanley Matthews, the great soccer player of post-war years, and Don Everly, of the Everly Brothers close harmony duo, were born on this day.

2. Candlemas has always been considered specially fortunate for the birth of a child, and churches used to hold special services to bless mothers and Candlemas babies. It is the birthday of President Giscard d'Estaing of France.

3. The feast day of St Blaise, a holy man who was said to be able to cure illnesses in both men and animals. The day is still regarded as a time to ask for divine help for throat troubles, and churches all over the world hold ceremonies for blessing the throat. On this day in Hamburg in 1809 Felix Mendelssohn was born. One of his many beautiful musical compositions has become linked with marriage: *The Wedding March*.

4. A day of celebration for the people of Sri Lanka, which became independent on February 4, 1948, changing its name from Ceylon. Charles Lindbergh, the first man to make a solo flight non-stop across the Atlantic; Norman Wisdom, the comedian; and Alice Cooper (real name Vincent Furnier), leader of one of the top US pop bands, were born on this date.

5. Bells often ring out on this day in honour of St Agatha, the patron saint of bellfounders and bellringers. Loaves of a special shape used to be baked on her feast day, and in some churches bread is still blessed in her honour. You share your birthday with Frank Muir, radio writer and broadcaster.

6. Princess Elizabeth became Queen on this day in 1952 on the death of her father, George VI. It is New Zealand's National Day. Among the birthday people are Denis Norden, writing partner of yesterday's birthday celebrant, Frank Muir; Gayle Hunnicut, the actress; Ben Lyon, one of the recent past's great film and radio stars; and Freddie Trueman, the cricketer.

7. The birthday of one of the most successful English novelists who ever lived: Charles Dickens. You can see the room in which he was born in Commercial Road, Portsmouth. It is also the anniversary for Hattie Jacques, who acts in a popular TV comedy series with Eric Sykes.

8. The new Elizabethan age was born on this day in 1952, when Elizabeth II took the oath of accession as Queen of Great Britain and Head of the Commonwealth. It is the anniversary of the birth of Robert Burton in 1577, a noted philosopher and author of *The Anatomy of Melancholy*. He had a great belief in astrology, calculating from the horoscope of his birth that he would die when he was sixty-two – which he did.

9. The feast day of St Apollonia, the patron saint of dentists, and of anyone with toothache. Today in Italy any sufferer will probably visit a church and light a candle in the saint's honour, *en route* to the dentist. Those born on this day are supposed to have good teeth for all their lives.

10. The birthdate of Harold Macmillan, Britain's Prime Minister 1957–1963; of Mary Rand, gold-, silver- and bronze-medal winning Olympic athlete; and Larry Adler, the harmonica player.

11. If it is cold today don't be surprised. February 11 often marks a cold spell, and in 1895 it was the coldest day ever known in Britain, – 27·2 deg. Centigrade, recorded at Braemar in Scotland. Two great inventors were born on this day – Thomas Edison, who held a thousand patents for his inventions, including the gramophone, megaphone, incandescent lamp, and telegraph systems; and William Fox Talbot, pioneer in photography.

12. In France and southern Europe this is Lemon Day, when the fruit is gathered. The legend is that on this day, after Eve had been banished from the Garden of Eden, she arrived at Menton in southern France and planted a lemon pip she had brought with her from Eden; from the tree that grew from that pip all lemon trees have since originated. In places where lemons are cultivated there are processions and dancing in the streets in celebration. This is the birthdate of Abraham Lincoln, the boy who was born in a miserable log cabin and became President of the USA; of Charles Darwin, the naturalist who wrote *The Origin of Species,* which gave the world the theory of the evolution of all living things; and of General Omar Bradley, Second World War American general in command of the US forces liberating Europe.

13. The birthday of Georges Simenon, author of the detective novels featuring Inspector Maigret and many other stories, totalling in all 514 books, of which more than 300 million copies have been sold.

14. St Valentine's Day, when birds are supposed to choose their mates and young people send their secret messages to those they love. Back in Roman times boys and girls celebrated this day as the festival of youth, and drew lots to see who their partners for the festivities should be. Despite the name, the saint whose feast day this is has nothing to do with the romantic activities of February 14.

15. The birthday of our money – on this day in 1971 the old pounds, shillings and old pence were replaced by pounds and new pence. It is also the birthday of Galileo, father of physical science and astronomer, who was the first man to proclaim that the earth moved round the sun, the moon had mountains and valleys, there were spots on the sun, and the Milky Way consisted of millions of stars.

16. The birthday of Sir Geraint Evans, Welsh opera singer. It is

the anniversary of the birth of G. M. Trevelyan, whose books on English history are in every school library.

17. St Fintan's day. This Irish saint lived very simply, eating only vegetables and fruit, tilling the soil with simple tools, and never using any animal to help with the farm work. The monks under his supervision lived in the same way. Many modern communes of young people, and those who prefer the simple life, make Fintan their patron.

18. The birthday of Yoko Ono, Japanese wife of John Lennon, and vocalist with the Plastic Ono Band.

19. Prince Andrew, second son of the Queen, was born on this day. His other names are Albert Christian Edward, and many boy babies born on the same day as he was in 1960 were given one of these names.

20. The anniversary of a day which brought peace to the world when in 1783 the opposing armies of Britain and the USA finally laid down their arms. It is the feast day of St Ulric, who lived in Somerset, where sportsmen and hunters regard him as their patron saint.

21. The birthday of Douglas Bader, who lost both legs in a flying accident before the Second World War, but rejoined the RAF and flew as a fighter pilot in the Battle of Britain. His aircraft was later shot down but he bailed out safely, and was taken prisoner by the Germans who agreed that a new pair of artificial legs could be dropped by the RAF for their famous comrade.

22. Both Sir Robert and Lady Baden-Powell, founders of the Boy Scout and Girl Guide movements, were born on 22nd February. It is also the birthdate of George Washington, the first president of the USA; Frederic Chopin, Polish composer and pianist; and the Duchess of Kent, whose forenames are Katharine Lucy Mary.

23. Samuel Pepys, who kept a diary filling more than 3000 pages closely written in a code which was not studied and understood for more than a hundred years, was born on this day in 1633.

24. The feast day of St Matthias, chosen by lot to join the twelve apostles after Judas Iscariot was expelled. Because of the saint's good fortune in this decision by chance his day is regarded as a lucky one for such speculative activities as buying Premium Bonds or playing games where skill does not really count. This was the birthday of Wilhelm Grimm, who with his brother wrote the famous fairy tales.

25. A trio of well-known birthdays: John Arlott, radio and TV cricket commentator; Victor Sylvester, veteran leader of a band playing in strict tempo for dancing; and George Harrison, former lead guitarist with the Beatles and subsequently a soloist with his own record label.

26. Victor Hugo, one of France's greatest novelists, author of *Les Misérables*, was born on this day in 1802. It is also the birthday of Johnny Cash, American country music's most successful vocalist.

27. Three anniversaries: Henry Longfellow, the American poet who wrote *Hiawatha*; film star Elizabeth Taylor, who began her career at the age of thirteen; and Steve Harley (whose real name is Steven Nice), vocalist with the Cockney Rebel group.

28. The feast day of St Oswald, who was bishop of Worcester in the tenth century and still remembered there for his kindness to the people of the town; he died while serving poor and hungry people at his table.

29. If Leap Year birthdays come only once every four years they are by tradition of special importance, it being said that whatever qualities the brothers and sisters of a leap year baby may have, the February 29 birthday celebrant has them fourfold. Rossini, who wrote thirty-eight operas, of which *The Barber of Seville* is the best known; Joss Ackland, the actor, and James Ogilvy, son of Princess Alexandra and the Honourable Angus Ogilvy, were all born on February 29.

February

Birthday Dates	16
1	17
2	18
3	19
4	20
5	21
6	22
7	23
8	24
9	25
10	26
11	27
12	28
13	29
14	
15	

March

It is easy to understand why March for many centuries was the first month of the year. Every day the mornings start earlier and twilight comes later. And if at the beginning March 'comes in like a lion', with strong cold winds, it usually 'goes out like a lamb', mild and calm, though an old proverb that March always borrows three good days from April to mislead us about improving weather is often proved by a sudden return to snow and frost.

Apart from those years in which Easter falls in March (it can be as early as March 22) there is only one great festival day in the month – Lady Day on March 25 – though it does not give much cause for celebration for our mums and dads, with bills to pay. This date is a quarter day when debts are due to be paid.

If you believe in fairies, as most people, young or old, used to do in olden times, twilight and midnight on the evening and night of March 25 are supposed to be the best times to see the Little People. It helps if the night brings a full moon. According to those who wrote down their experiences the best places to see fairies are in the branches of trees or on rough ground where there are holes and crevices down which the fairies can disappear. They always seem to be dressed in green – which must make them very difficult to see!

In woods and fields, and even in town areas, March is certainly the month of new life. March 21 or 22 marks the beginning of spring by the definition of astronomers, when the day and night are of equal length all over the world, though south of the equator it is of course the start of autumn.

In the Northern hemisphere animals and insects which have slept the winter away emerge – spiders, butterflies, wasps, bees, hedgehogs and dormice among them. Hares show off to attract a mate by leaping and rushing about – 'mad as a March hare'. The first of the birds which left Britain in the autumn return – swallows, martins, wheatears, chiff-chaffs, and cuckoos. And our winter visitors such as redwings, fieldfares, snipe and teal prepare to depart.

Hedges turn green and buds can be seen on chestnut and sycamore. Apart from tulips, narcissi and daffodils, most of which grow from imported and cultivated bulbs, there are still a few places where wild daffodils grow, and everywhere daisies, dandelions and marsh marigolds burst into bloom.

If your birthday falls in March you share the birth month with many, many others. In Britain more babies are born in March of the average year than in any other month.

March

1. St David's Day, the festival in honour of Wales's national saint, known in Welsh as Dewi. Today many Welsh people and Welsh regiments wear the saint's emblem, a leek, though no one knows why the name of St David is connected with the plant; others wear a daffodil which in Welsh is Cenin Pedr, (St Peter's leek). Two notable birthdays: David Niven, film star, and Glenn Miller, conductor of a dance band popular during the Second World War.

2. The feast day of St Chad, a saintly man who always travelled on foot, so that in the north of England, where he was born and worked, he is regarded as the patron saint of walkers and tramps.

3. The anniversary of the birth of Kenneth Grahame, author of

The Wind in the Willows which is also known as a play, *Toad of Toad Hall*, and of Ronald Searle, the artist famous for his cartoons of, among other things, the schoolgirls of St Trinians.

4. A memorable anniversary for those who go down to the sea in ships, for on this day in 1824 the Royal National Lifeboat Institution was founded, and for the first time those in danger from shipwreck and disaster around Britain's coasts had a chance of rescue. In 1801 Thomas Jefferson became President of the USA, taking the oath of office in Washington, the first President to be inaugurated there. It is the birthday of Patrick Moore, the TV astronomer.

5. The anniversary of the birth of Lord Beveridge, who in 1942 gave the government a plan for providing everyone with help when they were ill, unemployed, or otherwise in need of aid; in effect he created the welfare state in which all British people now live.

6. Elizabeth Barrett Browning, the poet, was born on this day in 1806. Today is also the birthday of David Sheppard, former England cricketer and later the Bishop of Liverpool.

7. Sir Edwin Landseer, who began sketching horses and cattle from life at the age of six and became the most famous painter of animals of his day, was born on March 7, 1802. He made the design for the lions which crouch below Nelson's statue in Trafalgar Square. It is also the anniversary of Joseph Niepce, the inventor of photography, and the birthday of Lord Snowdon.

8. 'Happy Birthday' was sung on this day in 1969 by the astronauts floating in space in Apollo IX. This song, now an essential part of everyone's birthday celebrations, was first published in 1935 and is probably the most widely and frequently sung tune ever written.

9. The birth anniversary of the man who gave his name to the New World: Amerigo Vespucci, who began exploring the

coast of the new lands seven years after Columbus discovered them, but his accounts were so widely read in Europe that people began calling it 'Amerigo's country', and the name was soon changed to Amerigo and then America.

10. Prince Edward, third son of Queen Elizabeth II, was born this day in 1964. Two historic anniversaries: 'Mr Watson, come here, I want you', an order spoken by Alexander Graham Bell in his laboratory on March 10, 1876, was the first sentence spoken over a telephone. And on this day in 1906 the first deep underground railway, London's Bakerloo line, was opened.

11. The birthday of Jessie Matthews, in the years before the war Britain's best-loved star in musical films.

12. The feast day of St Gregory the Great. He was Pope in the seventh century and the man known for the occasion when he saw three fair-haired, blue-eyed boys in a Roman slave market and asked who they were. 'They are Angles from the islands of Britain,' he was told. 'Not Angles, but angels,' St Gregory replied; 'they have angelic faces.' As a result of meeting these boys he began to arrange for missionaries to go to pagan England.

13. In 1847 this was a unique birthday for a little girl – the first baby in Britain to be born while her mother was pain-free under chloroform. The grateful parents named her Anaesthesia. It is the birthday of boxer Joe Bugner.

14. The anniversary of the birth of Albert Einstein, propounder of the theory of relativity which proved that time and space are not absolute, but relative to the observer. After he published his theory in 1921 all work of mathematicians and physicists was affected, and the production of nuclear power made possible.

15. The Ides of March. The Romans had names for two of the days in each month, Nones and Ides, based on the number of the day instead of its name in the week. As Shakespeare tells in his play *Julius Caesar*, the Emperor was warned to 'beware the Ides of March,' and on this day he was assassinated in 44 B.C. On a

happier note, it is the feast day of St Zachary, an eighth-century Pope who freed slaves and looked after the poor of Rome.

16. The anniversary of the birth of Matthew Flinders, who between 1798 and 1803 made the first surveys of the coasts of Australia. If German farmers are worried at this period by lack of spring rains they choose today to invoke St Heribert, who in 1021 was begged by the people of Cologne to pray for the ending of a drought. As his prayers ended torrential rain fell over the whole district.

17. St Patrick's Day, when every Irishman likes to wear a bunch of shamrock, and all Irish soldiers in the British army are allowed to wear the plant on their uniforms in honour of Irish soldiers' gallantry during the Boer War. The reason for the shamrock being the national emblem of Ireland is that St Patrick is said to have picked the three-leaf plant to illustrate the meaning of the Trinity – three Gods in One. This is the birthday of Rudolf Nureyev, who was born in 1939 on a train crossing Russia.

18. The feast day of a saint who was also a king -- Edward the Martyr, who was assassinated when he was only sixteen. He is supposed to watch over those who have suffered injustice. A happier anniversary is that on this day in 1965 the Russian astronaut Leonov became the first man to leave his space capsule and walk in space.

19. The anniversary of the birth of two great explorers: David Livingstone, born in 1813, who penetrated deep into Africa; and Sir Richard Burton, who explored the lake regions of equatorial Africa with John Hanning Speke.

20. St Cuthbert's day; he was a saint who was a shepherd boy in Northumberland and later lived among the birds on the islands of Lindisfarne and Farne, so he is regarded as the patron saint of naturalists and ornithologists. It is the anniversary of the birth of Henrik Ibsen, the Norwegian poet and playwright, best known for his plays *A Doll's House* and *The Wild Duck*.

21. The Vernal Equinox, when night and day are of the same length, and the first day of spring. It is the feast day of St Benedict, who founded one of the greatest of the world's monasteries, at Cassino in Italy.

22. The birthday of Nicholas Monsarrat, novelist; he wrote the popular award-winning book *The Cruel Sea*.

23. The birthday of Roger Bannister, the first man to break the four-minute time for running the mile in 1954 and a record breaker in the Empire and European Games of that year. He retired from athletics to concentrate on his work as a doctor.

24. One of the best loved members of the Royal Family is remembered on this day: Queen Mary, who died in 1953. It is St Gabriel's day, commemorating the time when Mary was told she would give birth to Jesus. For centuries wives have regarded knowing on this day that they were soon to have a baby as a special blessing.

25. Lady Day, marking the end of the first quarter of the year. It is the anniversary of the birth of Arturo Toscanini, one of this century's great musical conductors, of whom famous operatic artistes like to say 'I sung under the baton of Toscanini' as proof of their success. Elton John (real name Reginald Kenneth Dwight) was born on this day in 1947; he started work as a tea boy in a music publishers. Other birthdays: Patrick Troughton, the actor who has appeared in many TV thrillers and plays, and a former 'Dr Who'; and John Laurie, one of TV's *Dad's Army*.

26. Diana Ross, first a singer with the Primettes and then with the Supremes, was born on this day in 1944.

27. The birthday of James Callaghan, who became Britain's Prime Minister in 1976, and the anniversary of the birth of Frederick Henry Royce in 1863. With his partner Charles Rolls he started the famous firm of engine builders.

28. A day of thanksgiving for the people of Spain: the anniversary of the end of the terrible civil war in 1939. Birthdays: Queen Ingrid, mother of the Queen of Denmark; Flora Robson, famous as an actress portraying Elizabeth I; and Dirk Bogarde, film actor.

29. The anniversary of the day in 1867 that Canada became a Dominion. It is the birthday of Sir William Walton, the composer. He has written many operas, the *Te Deum* for the coronation of Elizabeth II, and piano duets for children to play.

30. The anniversary of the birth of two world-famous painters: Vincent van Gogh, perhaps best known for his painting 'Sunflowers', seen in reproduction in innumerable homes; and of Francisco Goya, the Spanish artist who painted portraits and pictures showing the horrors of war.

31. Every school pupil who learns chemistry knows the man who was born this day in 1811: R. W. von Bunsen, who invented the gas burner which bears his name. It is the anniversary of the day in 1949 when Newfoundland joined the Dominion of Canada.

March

Birthday Dates	16
1	17
2	18
3	19
4	20
5	21
6	22
7	23
8	24
9	25
10	26
11	27
12	28
13	29
14	30
15	31

April

It's wise to keep in mind the date as April approaches, for it is probable that someone will try to play a practical joke on you on April 1, All Fools' Day. The proper sort of trick is to send someone on a fool's errand, such as going to a numbered house in a street, the victim discovering there is no such number, or pretending the postman has brought a letter when he hasn't. But the deception must start and finish before midday or the trickster it supposed to pay a forfeit.

No one really knows when April 1 first became a joker's holiday. One belief is that it is the feast day of Lud, the pagan god of fun and good humour, once worshipped by the Irish and Welsh. Another theory is that the day commemorates the time when Jesus was sent hither and thither between the high priests Annas and Caiaphas, and from Pontius Pilate to King Herod. Our ancestors liked to act out incidents in religious stories in this way and meant no disrespect.

Usually Easter falls in April and is both an anniversary as important as Christmas to Christians and a general celebration of the re-birth of the natural world around us. The name comes from that of the Norse goddess of spring, Eostre, with an egg her symbol of new life.

Today our Easter eggs are mostly of chocolate, or of cardboard with a gift inside. But really they should be real eggs, specially decorated for breakfast on Easter Sunday or boiled hard and used for various games.

The easiest way to colour an Easter pace egg, as it is called, is to wrap it in onion skins and boil it till it is hard; the shell will then be covered with a golden pattern. Or the egg can be painted with water colours after the yolk and white have been removed through two small holes. If you visit the Wordsworth museum at Grasmere in the Lake District you can see an array of beautifully decorated Easter pace eggs given to the poet's little daughter, Dora.

The last hours of April are, to the people of Europe, the time when witches fly through the air on their brooms. It is called Walpurgis night. They have to be back in their houses before midnight, when a new month is born.

In the countryside April is a lovely month. Charlock, wild violets, cowslips and primroses are all in flower. Thousands of migratory birds are arriving and all birds are building nests.

But April is also a fickle month, with rain as likely as sun, frosts as probable as serene, sunny days. Farmers don't like April to rush too fast towards summer because warmth encourages green growth and blossom only to be spoiled by later cold, while too many dry days wither tiny seedlings. 'April wet, good wheat' and 'A cold April brings us good bread and wine' are old proverbs just as true today as they were centuries ago.

April

1. A birthday on All Fool's Day does not mean you were born a fool – far from it. Those with this birth date are specially privileged to devise ingenious and successful tricks to make others April Fools. You share the date with the Royal Air Force, which came into being in 1918: within six months it was the most powerful air force in the world. This was also the birthday of Edgar Wallace, who was an orphan as a child, and became a famous author of thrillers. Like so many April 1 people he had tremendous energy and wrote 150 novels as well as many plays.

2. On this day an event occurred which is in all the history books. At the sea battle of Copenhagen in 1801 an naval officer ignored an order to break off the attack and thereby won a victory, gaining himself undying fame. He was Horatio Nelson, and he looked at the signal from the flagship by putting his telescope to his blind eye so that he could genuinely say that he never knew about the order.

3. If you live in Sussex or Hampshire you may know that this day is observed in honour of St Richard of Chichester, who was bishop in that town in the thirteenth century. He was famous for his kindnesses and generosity to poor people.

4. You share your birthdate with Jimmy Logan, the Scots entertainer, famous for his appearances in pantomimes. Boys born on this day used to be given the name of Ambrose, in honour of the saint whose feast day this is. St Ambrose lived in Italy in the fourth century when the Roman Empire was still powerful and its citizens were being converted to Christianity. Thanks to him church services are full of melody: he was the first bishop to encourage the writing and singing of hymns as a way for ordinary people to praise God.

5. One of the great benefactors of mankind was born on this day – Joseph Lister, the first surgeon to realise that harmful bacteria floated in the air, and wounds had to be carefully cleansed and protected. The first patient he successfully treated was a small Glasgow boy, James Greenless, with a leg broken after being run over. Disinfected dressings of oiled silk kept the germs at bay, and young James recovered perfectly. You also share this birthday with John le Mesurier, famous as Sergeant Wilson in the TV programme *Dad's Army*.

6. On this day 1909 an American, Robert Peary, reached the North Pole, the first time a human being had ever been there. His exploit is an example of the way 'try-try-try-again' can bring success. For twenty years he explored the Arctic on foot and by

dog sledge, probing farther and farther towards his goal. Once he spent four years on an expedition, trying to find a way over the drifting ice and enduring the terrible storms.

7. It's appropriate that England's greatest writer of poetry about flowers and natural beauty, William Wordsworth, should have been born on this springtime day in 1770. At this time of the year most of us recall:

> . . . A host of golden daffodils;
> Beside the lake, beneath the trees,
> Fluttering and dancing in the breeze.

April 7 is also a great anniversary date for Europe. In 1814 Norway was 'born' as an independent nation, and in 1904 Britain and France abandoned centuries of enmity and became friends once again by means of the Entente Cordiale (friendly understanding).

8. Have you ever heard of the world's sweetheart? She was Mary Pickford, the first of the world famous film stars, and born on this day in 1893. Tens of thousands of girls born on April 8 during the many years when films were silent were named Mary, yet the star's real name was Gladys Smith.

9. On this day in 1969 the supersonic era dawned when Concorde made its first flight – a short one from Bristol to Fairford, Gloucestershire. It is the birthdate of a trio of famous people: Isambard Brunel, who built bridges, canals, railways, and steamships; his *Great Western* was the first steamship to make regular crossings of the Atlantic, and *Great Britain* and *Great Eastern* were the largest ships built till then; Paul Robeson, the greatest negro singer in modern times; and Anne Miles, the unrivalled British netball player.

10. A good maxim for everyone is by William Hazlitt, born today: 'The art of pleasing consists in being pleased'. Think about it when talking to older folk, teachers, and your friends, and you'll realise it is very true. This was a historic day for millions of Americans who happened to be black, when the US Civil Rights Bill was passed in 1960.

11. This is the feast day of St Guthlac, who lived as a hermit on the site of Crowland Abbey in Lincolnshire, a holy place erected in his honour by King Ethelbald, ruler of that part of England called Mercia in the eighth century. St Guthlac was a great lover of birds and wild creatures which became so tame that they were always around his cell, sharing his food.

12. Another step forward for man on this date. Major Yuri Gagarin of the Soviet Union became the first spaceman to orbit the earth in 1961 when he went up in a six-ton satellite. Today is the birthday of Bobby Moore, West Ham's most famous soccer star, and David Cassidy, a major pop star in his mid-teens.

13. Many people with this birthdate have proved it is certainly not an unlucky one. It is the birthday of Sir Robert Watson-Watt, the Scots scientist who was the principal inventor of radar. Another famous inventor of many years before was Robert Trevithick, pioneer builder of railway steam engines. Two famous Americans also share this birthday: Thomas Jefferson,

who wrote the Declaration of Independence and became the country's third President, making Washington the capital; the other was a young man who thought of the idea of opening a shop where everything cost either five or ten cents. His name was Frank Woolworth.

14. The birthday of Sir John Gielgud, one of our great actors. To Americans it is a sad day, for on April 14, 1865, their President and national hero Abraham Lincoln was assassinated by an actor who fired into his box while the President was watching a play. It is the birthday of Ritchie Blackmore, the guitarist who formed the Deep Purple group.

15. If you enjoy modern music you will be happy to share this birthdate with Bessie Smith, known to everyone who appreciates modern music as the Uncrowned Empress of the Blues.

16. It seems that people born on this date have a sense of humour and acting ability, for it is the birthday of Charlie Chaplin, Spike Milligan, and Peter Ustinov. It is also the birthdate of Sir John Franklin, a famous seaman and explorer, who discovered the North West passage in the Arctic regions from the Atlantic to the Pacific. Today is the feast day of St Bernadette, whose birthplace of Lourdes in south-west France has since become one of the world's great centres of pilgrimage.

17. The birthday of John Ford, a Devonshire man who was doubtless encouraged by meeting Shakespeare to try his hand at writing poems and plays. Unfortunately some of his plays have been lost, but he was one of the great dramatists along with Shakespeare during the reign of Elizabeth I.

18. It is not often that a death is the cause for rejoicing, but it was on this day when Lord (Judge) Jeffreys died in the Tower of London. He was notorious for his cruel verdicts, sentencing more than 300 people to death and 1000 to slavery when he presided over the Bloody Assize. A much happier anniversary

is observed in Ireland, where the Republic of Eire was proclaimed in 1949.

19. This is Primrose Day, not only because this British flower is in full bloom by now but as a political festivity in honour of Benjamin Disraeli, Lord Beaconsfield, whose favourite flower it was. In the USA it is the anniversary date of the outbreak of the War of Independence in 1775, with the defeat of the British at Lexington and Concord. It is the birthday of British tennis star Sue Barker.

20. The feast day of St Agnes, an Italian who spent all her life as a nun in the Dominican order. She was gentle, kind and regarded as a worker of miracles. She rejected riches and power, living a life of great poverty. A pity her example was not followed by someone very different born on this day: Adolf Hitler.

21. Princess Elizabeth was born on this date in 1926, though since she became Queen she has had her official birthday celebrations in June. It is also the anniversary of Charlotte Brontë, born in 1816. The eldest of three famous sisters, Charlotte wrote the Brontë's best known novel, *Jane Eyre*.

22. The birthday of two famous – if very different – musicians. Yehudi Menuhin, probably the world's greatest violinist of the present time, was a skilful player at the age of four and playing in important concerts by the age of eleven. Peter Frampton, pop musician, was appearing as a guitarist and singer while still in his early teens. He had his own band, can play guitar, piano, drums and organ, and in both the USA and Britain has been regularly in the charts since 1975.

23. The feast day of St George, patron saint of England, soldiers and boy scouts. No exact details of his life in the third century are known, but the story that he rescued a maiden from a fierce animal – a dragon perhaps – in Libya has been told ever since the Crusaders returned from the Holy Land with the story. It is the birthday of the most famous child film star ever: Shirley

Temple, who earned more than £200,000 in the films she began making at the age of five.

24. You share your birthdate with a newspaper: the first issue of the *Daily Express* was published on this day in 1900. It is also the anniversary of the birth of Arthur Benson, famous for writing the words for *Land of Hope and Glory*, with music by Sir Edward Elgar, sung on the last night of the Promenade concerts. In Canterbury, especially, this feast day in honour of St Mellitus is celebrated. He was Archbishop of Canterbury in A.D. 607 and built a church, part of which can still be seen in the walls of the cathedral.

25. This is Anzac Day, observed in Australia and New Zealand in memory of the heroism of their soldiers who fought at Gallipoli in Turkey during the First World War. A trio of famous people to share your birthdate: Oliver Cromwell, Lord Protector of England; Marconi, principal inventor of radio; and Ella Fitzgerald, America's best loved negro vocalist.

26. This date is not the anniversary of William Shakespeare's birth, which is unknown, but on April 26, 1564, a clerk wrote in the register of baptisms at the parish church at Stratford-on-Avon: 'Gulielmus Filius Johannes Shakespere' (William son of John Shakespeare), and so this day is usually regarded as the famous playwright's birthday.

27. When Samuel Morse, born on this date in Charlestown, USA, experimented in 1832 with chemicals and electricity as a change from his work as a sculptor, he could not have known that one day his name would be linked with a code which could put the whole world into instant communication. His simple idea of devising a table of letters of the alphabet turned into dots and dashes enabled buzzers, bells, and lights to transmit messages.

28. A great date for Australians: on this day in 1770 Captain Cook discovered Botany Bay, and so named it because of the great variety of flowers and plants he found there. There is a

monument to mark the historic spot where he and his crew landed. Some years later – in 1789 – another historic event took place in the southern seas. Captain Bligh, once a fellow officer with Cook, was set adrift by his mutinous crew in mid-ocean. He and his officers managed to survive on a voyage of 4000 miles in an open boat to reach safety.

29. Two distinguished men share this birthdate: the Duke of Wellington, famous soldier and victor in many battles, including Waterloo, was born in 1769. The Emperor of Japan was born in 1901; his birthdate is carefully recorded in Japanese records as have been those of all his ancestors right back to 100 B.C.

30. Many Americans celebrate today as an important anniversary. In 1803 the US Government bought Louisiana and New Orleans from the Spanish and French, in 1900 Hawaii became part of the United States, and in 1789 Washington became the nation's first President. Today in Holland Queen Juliana's subjects hold celebrations in honour of her birthday.

April

Birthday Dates	16
1	17
2	18
3	19
4	20
5	21
6	22
7	23
8	24
9	25
10	26
11	27
12	28
13	29
14	30
15	

May is the merry month of the year, and anyone born this month is supposed to have a happy disposition, with good luck his constant companion for all his days. May Day, the first of the month, is now best known as Labour Day in many countries, but its old purpose was to welcome the arrival of summer.

In the England of Elizabeth I, and for centuries afterwards, people used to go into the woods and fields during the previous night and bring back branches of hawthorn and birch, and all the wild flowers they could find to decorate their houses with the flowers and the may blossom. They piled the birch twigs and branches on the village green to make bonfires which blazed as dawn came. Long before this, the Romans did much the same thing in celebrations they called Floralia, and the Druids at their temples in stone circles and at places like Stonehenge lit fires and erected poles covered with flowers to honour their god Beltane and to greet the rising sun.

The crowning of the May Queen, who reigned for a day, was the sign for the start of dancing round a maypole. Nowadays maypoles, with their ribbons plaited by the dancers, are seen mostly in school playgrounds. Once they were in every town and village. There was a very tall one in London's Strand which was left in position for the whole year.

The other important date in May is Whitsun, which usually falls during the month. The name is really White Sunday. Parents used to dress their new babies in white to take them to church for christening. It was also a day for outings and feasts, when villagers spent their savings and ate up the remaining winter store of food, now that new crops were almost ready and there would be plenty of work on farms to earn money.

'Cast ne'er a clout till May be out' is an old warning about believing that with May cold weather has gone. Some people believe the saying means the end of the month, and others that only when the white flowers of hawthorn are in full blossom is it wise to leave off winter clothing. Anyway, May has a nasty habit of bringing a brief cold spell, usually on May 11, 12, and 13. All over Europe these three days are called the Days of the Ice Saints. This frosty snap often damages fruit buds and delicate plants which have grown too quickly.

But May is still a month of wild flowers – bluebells, butter-cups and clover, with masses of blossom on lilacs, apple and cherry trees, chestnuts and mountain ash. Martins and swallows are finishing their nests under the eaves of buildings, and the first of the fledglings – rooks and blackbirds among them – test their wings.

May

1. May Day, the traditional beginning of summer, is now Labour Day in many countries and marked as a public holiday, when workers' organisations hold street parades and meetings. It is the birthday of Lady Sarah Armstrong Jones, daughter of Lord Snowdon and Princess Margaret.

2. The birth date of Bing Crosby (real name Harry). Since he made his first record in 1926 more than 362 million of his discs have been sold.

3. On this day in 1841 New Zealand became a British colony. Richard D'Oyly Carte, who produced all the Gilbert and Sulli-van operas when they first were performed, was born on this

day in 1844. It is the birthday of Henry Cooper, the boxer, and James Brown, drummer, guitarist and soul singer.

4. Two notable birth dates: Joseph Whitaker, whose Almanack – a birthday book and much more besides – was first published in 1869 and has been issued every year since; and Thomas Huxley, one of the world's greatest naturalists, who was the first to make a scientific study of fossils.

5. The anniversary of the birth in 1818 of Karl Marx, founder of the political theory of communism and author of the famous work *Das Kapital*.

6. A stage in the growth of Canada to a great nation when, in 1791, the little-explored country was divided into two provinces of Upper and Lower Canada. On this day in 1954 Roger Bannister ran a mile in 3 minutes 59·4 seconds. It is the birth date of Sigmund Freud, the Austrian doctor who advocated the study of man's mind with psychoanalysis.

7. The anniversary of three great contributors to the world's literature and music: Robert Browning, the poet, born in 1812; Johannes Brahms, the composer, born in 1833; and Peter Tchaikovsky, composer of operas and such famous ballet music as that for *Swan Lake*, *The Sleeping Beauty*, and *The Nutcracker*, in 1840.

8. The anniversary of a wonderful day in 1945 – VE Day when fighting in Europe ended. The official ending of hostilities took place twenty-four hours later. In 1660 Charles II rode through cheering crowds in the streets of London to take his place as king after the period of rule by Cromwell. Two birthdays: David Attenborough, famous on TV for his films of wild animals and birds; and pop star Gary Glitter (real name Paul Gadd).

9. The Channel Islanders celebrate this as Liberation Day, when in 1945 the islands' occupation by the Germans ended – the only part of the British Isles to be invaded by the enemy. On this day in 1927 Australia officially got a new capital, when

Parliament House in Canberra was opened. J. M. Barrie, author of *Peter Pan*, was born on this day in 1860.

10. The feast day of St Antonino, often regarded as the patron of those in need, because in his life he never refused to give alms: when he had no money he gave away his food, clothes, and furniture. It is the birthday of Donovan (real name Donovan Leitch), who first attained pop music fame as the resident star of TV's *Ready Steady Go*.

11. The birthday of Irving Berlin, composer of hundreds of song hits for more than half a century, including *Alexander's Ragtime Band* and *I'm Dreaming of a White Christmas*.

12. The feast day of St Pancras, rather unfairly regarded as the bringer of a snap of frost, thus damaging crops, but also with a tradition of ensuring that promises made on his day would be kept whatever the circumstances. Florence Nightingale, 'the lady with the lamp', was born on this day in 1820; so was Edward Lear, author of humorous poems, including *The Owl and the Pussycat*.

13. The birthday of Stevie Wonder (real name Stephen Judkins), singer, harmonica player and soul music star. Blind from birth, he was only twelve when he made his first hit disc – *Fingertips*.

14. The anniversary of the birth of Thomas Gainsborough in 1727; he painted the most famous people of his day. His portrait of *Master Buttall*, now known as *The Blue Boy*, is one of the world's most famous paintings of a child.

15. Anniversary of the birth of the jet age; on this day in 1941 Britain's first jet-powered aircraft flew for twenty minutes from the RAF station at Cranwell. In 1859 was born Pierre Curie, discoverer with his wife, Marie, of two new elements, radium and polonium, radioactive substances which made possible the development of nuclear power.

16. The feast of St Ubald; the belief used to be that anyone born on this saint's day would be blessed with Ubald's virtue of patience and forebearance. It is the birthday of Olga Korbut, Russian gymnast and winner of two Olympic gold medals at the age of seventeen.

17. Your great- and great-great-grandparents knew this day as one of the most exciting of the time. In 1900 news came that after seven months of siege the South African town of Mafeking was relieved; the Colonel in command of the heroic defenders was Baden-Powell. It is the anniversary of the birth of Edward Jenner, the country doctor who discovered how to prevent smallpox by vaccination.

18. The birthday of two great personalities of the entertainment world: Margot Fonteyn, Britain's greatest modern ballerina, and Perry Como, the American vocalist.

19. The feast day of St Dunstan, in whose life the great abbeys of Glastonbury, Westminster, Bath and Exeter were founded or restored through his work and inspiration. Ever since he lived a thousand years ago the coronations of our kings and queens have been based on the ritual the saint devised for King Edgar. He is considered the saint of workers in metal, and schoolboys – the last because he himself was a well-loved master at a school in Canterbury.

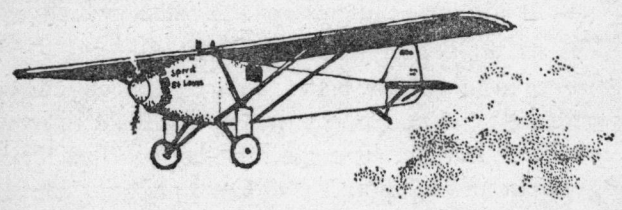

20. On this day in 1927 a young man named Charles Lindbergh took off from New York in an attempt to win a £25,000 prize for the first solo flight to Paris. It took him thirty-three hours – the first man to fly non-stop and alone between the New World and the Old. Today is the birthday of Joe Cocker (real name John Robert) once an apprentice gas fitter but a drummer and harmonica player at the age of fifteen, and later one of the best white singers of blues and soul music Britain has ever produced.

21. The anniversary of a day when, to the alarm of some people, Britain first 'played with time'. In 1916 a daylight saving law was brought into operation, with clocks altered one hour for summer time, now a routine annual event in this and many other countries. Elizabeth Fry, who devoted her life to getting better conditions in gaols for women prisoners was born on this day in 1780. Just under a century earlier, the day saw the birth of Alexander Pope, poet and author.

22. The anniversary of the birthdays of Richard Wagner, composer of some of the greatest operas ever written; Sir Arthur Conan Doyle, author of the Sherlock Holmes stories; Laurence Olivier, Britain's most illustrious modern actor, and George Best, soccer star.

23. The birthday of Denis Compton, Middlesex and England cricketer, who in 1947 scored eighteen centuries in one season, and in the following year made 300 in three hours' batting.

24. On this day in 1819 a baby named Alexandrina Victoria was born; she became Queen Victoria. On May 24, 1930, an aircraft touched down in Australia piloted by Amy Johnson. She had left England nineteen days before, and was the first woman to make a solo flight between the two countries.

25. The birth date of Ralph Waldo Emerson, American writer and poet, who was clever enough at the age of twelve to say goodbye to the school he was leaving with a little verse:

> This morning I have come to bid adieu
> To you my schoolmates and, kind Sir, to you.
> For six short months my lot has here been cast,
> And I think how pleasantly they've past.

26. Queen Mary, the grandmother of Elizabeth II, was born on this day in 1867. It is the feast day of St Augustine who in the year 597 landed in Kent with forty monks to begin the conversion of pagan England to Christianity.

27. The feast day of the Venerable Bede, born on this day in the year 673 in Northumberland. Almost all we know about England till the seventh century comes from the history book he wrote. He was a learned man in an age when few people could even read or write, and studied medicine, astronomy, and foreign languages. He was also the first English writer on the subject of the calendar.

28. One of the most unusual birthdays ever: on this day in 1934 at Callandar, Ontario, the Dionne quintuplets were born. They were named Yvonne, Annette, Emilie, Cecile and Marie. The day is the anniversary of the birth of William Pitt the Younger in 1759, who became Prime Minister of Britain; and of Ian Fleming, author of the James Bond stories.

29. Royal Oak Day, commemorating both the birthday of Charles II and the occasion when he successfully eluded the Roundhead soldiers pursuing him by hiding in an oak tree. On this day in 1953 men first stood on the summit of Mount Everest – the New Zealander Edmund Hillary and his Sherpa guide Tensing Norkhay. It is the anniversary of the birth of John Kennedy, former president of the USA.

30. The feast day of St Joan of Arc, 'The Maid of Orleans' and France's greatly loved heroine. It is also the festival of St Felix, a Roman. In Europe many boys and girls born on this day are named Felix or Jeanne (Joan).

31. Anniversary of the birth of William Heath Robinson, whose illustrations for Hans Andersen's fairy tales and *The Arabian Nights* are to be found in many editions of these books, but he was best known for his humorous drawings of complicated machines built for the simplest purpose.

ADDING THE FINAL PING TO THE FLAVOUR

TESTING THE PIQUANCY OF A NEW BREW OF CHUTNEY SAUCE

May

Birthday Dates	16
1	17
2	18
3	19
4	20
5	21
6	22
7	23
8	24
9	25
10	26
11	27
12	28
13	29
14	30
15	31

June

The red-letter day of the month comes on June 24, which by tradition is Midsummer Day, even though in most years the sun rises and sets at the same time for two or even three days before that date.

We don't mark Midsummer Eve and Day with much fuss nowadays. In the past, when the weather decided whether people would eat well or almost starve, great celebrations took place to please the sun god and all the deities whom people venerated. Then the Christians made it a holy day, marking the birthday of St John the Baptist. Though the festivities remained much the same as in pagan times, they were now being blessed by the priest, with dancing round the village church.

Just before dawn – which comes only two hours after midnight – the last sticks and twigs used to be added to great bonfires. They were lit when the first gleam of sunshine lit up the sky. When the fires died down men, women, children and farm animals walked through the ashes in the belief that this would both bring good luck for twelve months ahead and ensure good health.

Then, with daylight, children went into the fields to gather St John's Wort, the golden-flowered weed which usually comes into bloom in mid-June. Bunches of the flowers were hung over the doors of every cottage to bring good fortune and prosperity.

The most ominous event was for rain to fall during the brief hours of darkness before Midsummer Day's dawn. The rain

73

was said to prevent the fairies coming out for one of their rare excursions into the real world. Girls who expected, if they went out secretly into the darkness, to be led by the little people to the house where their future husband lived, were disappointed.

June is usually quite a dry month – really the best month for holidays – and wet days in the month have always been regarded as a gloomy sign of a miserable summer and autumn.

> If on the eighth of June it rain
> It foretells a wet autumn, men sain.

Wet or fine, June is a flowery month, particularly for the queen of flowers – the rose. In France June 4 is rose day. Shows are held, and florists often give away a rose whatever other flowers are bought by the customer.

Even more lavish than the flowers of the wild rose in country hedgerows are the elder flower blossoms. Only when these masses of tiny white flowers are out is summer supposed to be really here – and it is over as soon as the flowers drop off and the elderberries turn black.

June

1. 'The Glorious First of June' was the name given to this day after the naval victory in 1794 of the Royal Navy fleet commanded by Admiral Lord Howe over the French. Sailors' sons born on this day are often named Richard, which was Lord Howe's Christian name. The day is the birthday of Frank Whittle, inventor of the jet engine for aircraft; and John Masefield, the poet who wrote wonderful verse about the sea and sailors.

2. The Coronation of Queen Elizabeth II took place on this day in 1953. Thomas Hardy, the author of stories about country life in the west of England, was born on June 2, 1840. Charlie Watts,

drummer with the Rolling Stones, is also a June 2 birthday boy.

3. Irish people celebrate this day as the feast of St Kevin, who founded a monastery at Glendalough in County Wicklow and built seven churches there; the valley is regarded as the most beautiful and holy in Ireland. Most Irish boys born on this day are given Kevin as one of their names. It was the birthday of George V, grandfather of Elizabeth II.

4. The wreck of a Dutch ship on June 4, 1629, had the accidental result of giving Australia its first European settlers, when two of the crew, a man and a boy, are believed to have got ashore on the west coast of Australia. Two centuries later light-skinned aborigines who told of white ancestors seemed to prove the two Dutch sailors survived and married into a native tribe.

5. The feast day of St Boniface, a Devonshire monk who spent most of his life in Germany, where this day is still an important occasion for services and pilgrimages to the monastery he founded at Fulda, near Kassel. It is the anniversary of the birth of Igor Stravinsky, the Russian composer who wrote the ballet music for *The Firebird* and *Petrushka*.

6. Just before dawn on this day in 1944 the greatest military invasion in history began when British, American and allied forces landed in Normandy and began the liberation of Europe from the Germans. Birthdays: Captain Robert Scott, the Antarctic explorer; and Sir Henry Newbolt, poet and author, best known for his poems about the sea.

7. The birthday of two world-famous singers and entertainers: Dean Martin and Tom Jones.

8. The anniversary of the birth of John Millais, the artist who painted the famous pictures *The Boyhood of Raleigh*, *Ophelia*, *Little Miss Muffet*, and also *Bubbles*, one of the first paintings ever used for advertising – in this instance for toilet soap.

9. George Stephenson, the engineer who built the Rocket steam locomotive and with his son launched the Railway Age the world over, was born on this day in 1781. It is also the birthday of Cole Porter, composer of innumerable song hits.

10. The Duke of Edinburgh's birthday. He was born in 1921. It is also Portugal's National Day.

11. When this day is a Saturday it is celebrated as the Queen's official birthday with the ceremony of Trooping the Colour, when the Queen carries out an inspection of her troops on Horse Guard's Parade in Whitehall. John Constable, the famous painter of English landscapes, was born on this day in 1776.

12. The anniversary of the birth of Charles Kingsley, who wrote *Westward Ho*!, an exciting account of Elizabethan sea-dogs, and the children's long-time favourite, *The Water Babies*.

13. W. B. Yeats, one of Ireland's greatest poets, was born on this day in 1865. It is also the anniversary of Thomas Arnold, who became headmaster of Rugby School and created the pattern of education and games soon copied by all public schools. Though he helped to make the game of rugby football well known it was played at the school three years before he was appointed head-master.

14. A historic date in the history of man's conquest of the air. On this day in 1919 John Alcock and Arthur Whitten Brown took off from Newfoundland and landed sixteen hours later in Galway, Ireland, the first men to make a non-stop crossing of the Atlantic by airplane. Harriet Beecher Stowe, author of *Uncle Tom's Cabin*, was born on this day in 1811. Today is also the birthday of Rod Argent, vocalist and pianist, who formed the the combo which bears his surname – Argent.

15. A great day for all the world's democracies and the freedom of ordinary people for nearly eight centuries. On June 15, 1215, King John signed the Great Charter (Magna Carta) which became the basis of the liberties of the common people of his kingdom.

16. The anniversary of the day in 1963 when the first woman went into space. She was a Russian, Valentina Tereshkova, and her space ship was called Vostok VI.

17. The feast day of St Harvey, the blind son of a British bard who lived in the sixth century. He roamed around the west of England and Brittany, in France, as a minstrel and monk. Many boys in Brittany are named Hervé after him, and in England the surname Harvey was originally adopted in the saint's honour.

18. The anniversary of one of the great battles of history when in 1815 the British, commanded by the Duke of Wellington, defeated the French under Napoleon at Waterloo. The fighting began at 11.30 a.m. and by nightfall it was all over, and a terrible war which had long been waged all over Europe came to an end. It is the birthday of pop star Paul McCartney.

19. The anniversary of the birth of James I, at first King of Scotland and then of Great Britain and Ireland. It is the feast day of St Juliana, who founded an order of nuns. White doves are supposed to be living symbols of her.

20. The birthday of Chet Atkins, the American guitarist who produced discs by such famous pop singers as Elvis Presley and Jim Reeves. In his native Tennessee he is known as 'the King of the Nashville Cats'.

21. Silver jubilees are quite often celebrated to mark twenty-five years of a British monarch's reign, but only once has there been a golden jubilee, which took place on this day in 1887 to celebrate Queen Victoria's reign of fifty years. This is the longest day of the year.

22. The feast day of St Alban, who lived in the third century in the town now named after him – St Albans. The spot where he died is marked by the great abbey standing on the hill on which the town is built.

23. St John's Eve, the summer solstice, when the sun seems to pause on the day it is farthest from the equator. To be born on this day used to be regarded as being blessed with long life. Len Hutton, the Yorkshire and England cricketer, and Adam Faith (real name Terence Nelham), one of the first modern teenage pop stars, were born on this day.

24. Midsummer Day, when daisies were once picked in great numbers and hung in bunches over house doors to bring good fortune. Many girls born on this day were given the name Daisy to ensure a lucky life. By tradition St John the Baptist was born on this day and it is celebrated as his feast day, with this name being given to boys born on June 24.

25. The anniversary of an event re-told in Western films and adventure stories, when in 1876 Colonel Custer and his men made their last stand at a place called Little Big Horn in Montana and were wiped out by Red Indian Sioux warriors led by Sitting Bull. This is the birthday of Cyril Fletcher, the 'odd ode' man.

26. The birthday of Georgie Fame (real name Clive Powell), pop singer and pianist who is often seen in TV commercials advertising coffee.

27. The feast day of a king who became a saint – Ladislas the First, King of Hungary. He is that country's national hero, and in most Hungarian families the eldest son is given the saint's name – in Hungarian 'Laszlo'.

28. The birthday of Eric Ambler, writer of many thrillers.

29. The anniversary of the birth in 1577 of Peter Paul Rubens, famous painter. This is the feast day of St Peter, whose body is believed to lie below the altar in the basilica of the Vatican in Rome. The saint has long been regarded as the patron saint of doctors; according to legend he had wonderful powers of healing so that even his passing shadow relieved pain.

30. The anniversary of one of the most amazing balancing feats ever made, when in 1859 a Frenchman named Jean Grandet (known as Blondin) walked on a rope 1100 ft long suspended 160 ft above Niagara Falls.

June

Birthday Dates	16
1	17
2	18
3	19
4	20
5	21
6	22
7	23
8	24
9	25
10	26
11	27
12	28
13	29
14	30
15	

July

If the first of July it be rainy weather,
'Twill rain, more or less, for four weeks together.

That old rhyme is ominous for those of us who are having an
early holiday, and by July 14 there is another dire prophecy:

St Swithin's Day, if thou dost rain,
For forty days it will remain.

St Swithin was a bishop who lived in Winchester nearly a
thousand years ago. He wanted to be buried in the churchyard
and is said to have made his prophecy about forty days of rain if
his wishes were not observed. They were not – his bones were
laid to rest in the cathedral. Ever since, people have believed rain
on his day will bring wet weather until the middle of August,
but they forget that St Swithin also said:

St Swithin's Day, if thou be fair,
For forty days 'twill rain nae mair.

July often has many rainy days, but it is also a warm period,
the hottest month of the year. It also brings the first signs of
autumn. Hay is cut, and fields of barley, wheat and oats are
turning yellow. In the hedgerows blackberries are forming, and
in orchards plums and the first apples are ready to eat. Birds are
not singing so often as they did, and many, with their fledglings

83

on the wing, desert the nests they so patiently built a few months before.

After July 3 we are in the Dog Days if we live north of the equator. They last until August 11. It is the time when Sirius, the dog star, is supposed to exert its influence on the world. The Greeks and Romans believed it was an unlucky time, when illnesses were prevalent, and they also thought that the star's light sent dogs mad. These beliefs were, of course, groundless. One reason for starting such alarming stories was to account for the brightness of Sirius at this time of the year. It is the brightest star we can see, and thirty times brighter than the sun.

Some nations have every reason to believe that July is a splendid month. The Canadians celebrate Dominion Day on July 1, and in the United States July 4, Independence Day, is the great holiday of the year, with processions, patriotic meetings, and family reunions. But the gayest national celebration of them all is in France on July 14, when military parades, dancing in the streets and fireworks mark the anniversary of the storming of the Bastille and the start of the French Revolution.

Lastly, a strange day: July 25. Just for twenty-four hours, it is said, the chicory plant ensures that anyone who walks around at night holding some of its leaves is invisible to everyone else. Anyone, even a thief, wanting to open a lock without a key could do so by rubbing the lock with a chicory leaf and prising the gap near the lock with a knife which had to be made of gold. Even with that expensive tool the magic was dangerous. One sound from the person picking the lock – and he would shortly afterwards lose all his wealth.

July

1. Canada's birthday. In 1867 Upper and Lower Canada, New Brunswick and Nova Scotia joined as one nation. Canadians celebrate it as Dominion Day. Louis Blériot, the first man to fly

an airplane across the English Channel, was born on this day in
1872.

2. The birthday of Lord Home. As Sir Alexander Douglas-Home
he was Britain's Prime Minister in 1963 and 1964.

3. The start of the Dog Days, the hottest period of the year.

4. The United States' great celebration in commemoration of
the birth of the nation when the Declaration of Independence
was adopted in Philadelphia in 1776, marking the emergence of
the USA as an independent state. House parties and local festivities are held at which decorations are in red, white and blue,
and bells are rung to imitate the ringing of the Liberty Bell,
which marked the original occasion. Famous Americans born
on this date were Nathaniel Hawthorne, author of many fine
novels, including *Tanglewood Tales*; Stephen Foster, composer
of negro songs such as *The Old Folks at Home*; and Louis
Armstrong, the great jazz musician.

5. People in the Isle of Man celebrate this as Tynwald Day to
commemorate the founding of the court of Tynwald, one of
the oldest law-making bodies in the world. It is the birthdate of
Cecil Rhodes, who gave his name to Rhodesia.

6. The birthday of Beatrix Potter, author of the famous stories
about Peter Rabbit, Squirrel Nutkin, Jemima Puddleduck and
many other animals. It is the feast day of St Godelive; the water
from the well at her home in Belgium is supposed to cure sore
throats.

7. The feast day of St Willibald, who was born in the west of England 1200 years ago, and is believed to have been the first Englishman to make a pilgrimage to the Holy Land; as he passed through Italy the people thought that a man making such a long journey must be a king, and to this day he is known to Italians as Richard, King of the English. Birthday people: Thomas Gray, the poet; Jon Pertwee, TV actor of 'Dr Who' fame; and Ringo Starr, the former Beatles' drummer.

8. The birthdate of John D. Rockefeller, who rose from his first job as an assistant book-keeper to become the world's richest man.

9. The feast day of two saints, John Fisher and Thomas More, both of whom incurred the anger of Henry VIII and were condemned to death in the Tower of London. The story of St Thomas was told in the film *A Man for All Seasons*. Today is the birthday of Edward Heath, Britain's Prime Minister 1970–1974.

10. The birthday of Ian Wallace, a noted singer and well known for his song about a hippopotamus – *Mud, Glorious Mud* – and of Virginia Wade, British tennis star.

11. John Quincy Adams, the sixth president of the United States, was born on this day in 1767.

12. Julius Caesar's birthdate in 102 B.C. The month of July was named after him to mark the event when he changed the calendar. It is also the feast day of St Veronica, who is said to have wiped the perspiration from the face of Jesus as he toiled on the road to Calvary with the Cross. The piece of linen is preserved in St Peter's, Rome. Many girls born on this day are named Veronica, which means veil.

13. The anniversary of the birth of John Clare, known as the Northamptonshire peasant poet. He began writing verses as a very small boy, and later joined a band of gipsies, learning their songs which he set down in his poems.

14. France's great holiday, commemorating the storming of the Bastille and the release of prisoners in 1789, which was the beginning of the French Revolution.

15. St Swithin's Day, with a prophecy that if it is wet there will be rain for a further forty days. It is the anniversary of the birth of Rembrandt, one of the greatest painters who ever lived. It is also the birth date of a man whose long life is exactly known: Pierre Joubert, a Canadian, born in 1701 and living for 113 years 124 days.

16. On this day in 1607 an organist and musician named John Bull is said to have played his new composition to King James I. It was our national anthem – *God Save the King*. Sir Joshua Reynolds, painter of portraits, was born today in 1723.

17. The feast day of a boy saint, Kenelm, who used to be regarded as the protector of small boys in the west of England where he lived his brief life as a prince, son of the king of Mercia. In Belgium the day is celebrated as the anniversary of the accession of their King Baudouin, who was only twenty-one when he succeeded to the throne.

18. The birthday of John Glenn, the astronaut who orbited the earth three times in *Friendship 7* (the number was to bring him good luck) travelling 81,000 miles in just under five hours. A famous cricketer has this birth date: W. G. Grace, who played in first class matches for forty-four seasons, scoring 54,896 runs and taking 2876 wickets.

19. The birth dates of Hilaire-Germaine Degas, French painter of ballet and circus scenes, and of A. J. Cronin, author of such books as *Hatter's Castle* and *The Stars Look Down*. The radio and TV series *Dr Finlay's Casebook* is based on Dr Cronin's stories.

20. The birthday of Sir Edmund Hillary, the New Zealander who was the first man to reach the top of Mount Everest. On this day in 1976 man took another great step forward in exploration when the *Viking 1* spacecraft landed on Mars.

21. On this day in 1969 the astronaut Neil Armstrong stepped off a short ladder to the surface of the moon; the first time any human being had walked on an extra-terrestial surface. It is the birthday of Ernest Hemingway, author of many best sellers, including *For Whom the Bell Tolls*; and Arthur Mee, first editor of the *Children's Encyclopaedia*.

22. This is often a very hot day; in 1868 the temperature reached 38·1°C (100·5°F), the hottest day ever recorded in England. Canadians celebrate this day as the greatest feat of exploration in the country's history, when in 1793 Alexander Mackenzie and his companions reached the sea at a spot north of what is now Vancouver, the first time white men had crossed the continent.

23. The birthday of Michael Foot, the politician, and of David Essex, pop singer and film star.

24. Alexander Dumas, the author of *The Three Musketeers* and *The Count of Monte Cristo*, was born on this day in 1803.

25. The feast day of St James, regarded as protector of fishermen and specially venerated in Spain, where great religious ceremonies are held on this day. The British court is still officially styled 'the Court of St James'. On this day in 1909 the Frenchman Blériot flew the English Channel in an aeroplane.

26. The birth dates of George Bernard Shaw, the famous playwright, and of Mick Jagger of the Rolling Stones.

27. Shirley Williams, MP for Hertford and Stevenage and the Minister for Education in 1976, was born on this day in 1930.

28. The feast day of St Samson, widely celebrated in Cornwall, the Scilly Isles, the Channel Islands and Brittany, where he worked as a monk in the sixth century. It is the birthday of cricketer Gary Sobers, who played for Nottingham.

29. Nurses, welfare workers, and those engaged in charitable work observe this day as the feast of St Martha, regarded as the patroness of all those who look after the needy and sick.

30. Henry Moore, the sculptor, was born on this day in 1898; he is considered the greatest of modern British sculptors. It is also the anniversary of the birth of Emily Brontë, the second of the three famous sisters, who wrote *Wuthering Heights*.

31. The feast day of St Neot, whose name was given to St Neot in Cornwall and St Neots in Huntingdonshire. He was a friend of King Alfred and recorded the famous story of King Alfred and the cakes.

July

Birthday Dates	16
1	17
2	18
3	19
4	20
5	21
6	22
7	23
8	24
9	25
10	26
11	27
12	28
13	29
14	30
15	31

August

If on August 1 you break off a piece of bread from a freshly baked loaf – it must still be hot from the oven – and make three wishes while you eat it, one of the wishes will be granted. You will not know which wish till later.

That's one of the old ceremonies of Lammas Day, the modern name for Hlaf maesse (Loaf Mass) of our Anglo-Saxon ancestors. It is also one of the oldest festivals of Christianity, once almost as eagerly awaited as Christmas or Easter.

On this day loaves were baked from the first yield of the corn harvest and taken to the church to be blessed. They were later given to the sick and poor. Then the harvesting could begin in earnest, everyone – men, women and children – going into the fields to help.

The kindly Spirit of the Harvest was believed to live among the corn stalks. She retreated farther and farther towards the centre of the field as the reapers advanced. No one wanted to be responsible for cutting down her last place of refuge, and lots were cast to see who must cut the last clump of corn. The stalks from it were gathered separately and made into a corn dolly – a little image of the spirit in plaited straw. The dolly was given pride of place at a harvest supper later in the month. Afterwards it was hung in the storage barn to bring good fortune to next year's crop of corn.

Corn dollies are still made in some country areas, and you can see old ones in many country museums.

Nowadays we commemorate this old feast day with an August Bank Holiday. Until recently this was on a Monday as close as possible to Lammas Day. The Harvest Festivals in our churches are also a memory of the old celebrations.

The other great festival of the month comes on August 15: the Feast of the Assumption, when the mother of Jesus was taken up to heaven. In many parts of Europe it is a national holiday. Little girls are dressed in white, and men and women wear a white flower. The day ends with family parties and dancing in the squares of towns and villages.

This is a quiet time for birds. Few of them sing any more, and some begin their annual migration. But it is the best month for butterflies. The most beautiful are on the wing, hatched out for their brief life before winter comes. Everywhere are the first signs of autumn, with fruits and berries ripening, and leaves on the trees becoming tinged with red, brown, and yellow.

Although August as a whole is not as hot as July, it often brings a few days which are the hottest of the year. There are frequent thunderstorms and bursts of torrential rain. With all the harvesting to be done country folk hope for day after day of fine weather. One proverb says:

> If the fourth of August be fair and clear,
> Then hope for a prosperous harvest that year.

August

1. Lammas Day, and for many farmers traditionally the first day of harvesting. Two great battles have this anniversary: Minden in 1759, known as the Battle of the Roses because the British and their allies fought and defeated the French through some rose gardens; and the Nile, in 1798, when Nelson defeated the French in Aboukir Bay and was created Baron Nelson of the Nile in honour of his victory. Another long battle of a different

kind ended on this day in 1834, when those who had fought for years against slavery saw its abolition ordered throughout the British Empire.

2. The anniversary of another stage in man's conquest of the earth: for the first time the summit of Mont Blanc was reached in 1787 by Horace Saussure, a Swiss mountaineer. On this day in 1858 British Columbia became a colony.

3. The start of a momentous voyage in 1492 when Columbus set sail from the port of Palos in Spain to find a sea route to Asia and thereby discovered America. It is the anniversary of Rupert Brooke's birth. He was famous for his poems about the First World War and on country life in peaceful England.

4. Queen Elizabeth the Queen Mother was born on this day in 1900. It is the anniversary of Britain declaring war on Germany in 1914.

5. Neil Armstrong's birthday; he was the first man on the moon. And the anniversary of the birth of Guy de Maupassant, French writer of novels and more than 260 short stories.

6. Alfred Tennyson, the poet, was born on this day in 1809. He wrote an immense number of poems, and most schoolchildren read *The Lady of Shalott*, *The Charge of the Light Brigade*, and the poems about King Arthur and his court. On this day in 1962 Jamaica became a new independent country.

7. The feast day of an unusual saint; among the good works of St Cajetan in Italy was his organisation of pawn shops, run to help those who needed to sell possessions to obtain some money; to Italians he is still the saint who will help them to find an honest lender or buyer.

8. The anniversary of the start of the Battle of Britain in 1940. On this day in 1870 an Act was passed to provide education for all boys and girls in England and Wales.

9. The anniversary of the birth in 1593 of Isaak Walton, the

writer of a book on fishing read by every enthusiastic angler ever since; and of Leonide Massine, Russian dancer and choreographer who devised and produced ballets, born in 1894.

10. Herbert Hoover, the thirty-first President of the U.S.A., was born on this day in 1874. It is the feast day of St Lawrence, regarded as protector of the poor and sick because when he was ordered by Roman officials to hand over the valuables in his church, he assembled the beggars and invalids he had been helping, saying, 'here are my church's treasures'.

11. The last of the Dog Days which began on July 3, and the end of a period once regarded as unhealthy because of the influence of Sirius the dog star.

12. Known among sportsmen as the Glorious Twelfth because on this day grouse shooting is legally permitted again.

13. The anniversary of the birth of John Logie Baird, the man who first demonstrated TV in Britain. He was fascinated by electricity from childhood, and in the street in Helensburgh, Scotland, where he lived as a boy wires criss-crossed the gardens and roadway with a telephone system he built before he was twelve.

14. John Galsworthy, the author of *The Forsyte Saga*, popular some years ago as a TV serial, was born on this day in 1867. It is the birthday of David Crosby, folk and rock singer.

15. The festival of the Virgin Mary, and in many parts of Europe a public holiday. Birthday anniversaries today include those of Princess Anne, born 1950; Napoleon, 1769; Walter Scott, the author of such great stories as *Kenilworth* and *Ivanhoe*, 1771, and T. E. Lawrence, 'Lawrence of Arabia', 1888. On this day in 1834 South Australia was named as a colony.

16. On August 16, 1960 Cyprus gained its independence.

17. After this date in 1836 everyone in Britain could be certain of their birth date, place of birth, and parentage, for registration of these details then became necessary by law. Before then, only church records existed, and many children were born who in later life never knew for sure the exact day of their birth or even their full names.

18. A historic birthday in 1587, when a baby girl, to be named Virginia Dare, was born to English parents in America – the first English child to start life in the New World. It is also the birthday of a very different 'New World' personality – film star Robert Redford.

19. Orville Wright, one of the brothers to build the first powered aircraft to fly, was born on this day in 1871. It is the birthday of Johnny Nash, soul and reggae vocalist.

20. The feast day of St Bernard, whose emblem is a beehive. In his lifetime he was known as the honeysweet teacher, and is often known as the patron of beekeepers and teachers.

21. The anniversary of the Battle of Bosworth, the last during the Wars of the Roses, when, according to Shakespeare's play, the defeated Richard III cried out, 'A horse! A horse! My kingdom for a horse' in a fruitless attempt to escape the vengeance of his enemy, the Earl of Richmond, who became Henry VII. This is the day in olden times when women were told to 'get candles anew', and they prepared waxes and fats to make candles for the darker evenings ahead. It is the birthday of Princess Margaret (christened Margaret Rose).

22. The anniversary of the birth of Sam Goldwyn, one of the most famous of film producers and the man who turned more actors and actresses into film stars than any other producer.

23. On this day in 1792 the French people found that the day and the month had been given entirely new names; the scheme did not work and was cancelled by Napoleon after fourteen years' trial. Scots people make this day a memorial to their hero William Wallace who was executed by his English enemies on August 23, 1305.

24. St Bartholomew's Day, when the first cold dew is said to appear with the dawn, heralding the beginning of autumn.

25. A day to be in Paris, when the people of the city celebrate the anniversary of their liberation in 1944 from German occupation, with parades and dancing in the streets. Appropriately it is also the feast day of France's saint-king, Louis XI, called the most perfect monarch the country ever had.

26. The anniversary of a historic battle, Crécy, in 1346, when the English and Welsh archers put the French enemy to rout. It was the first battle in a war which lasted a hundred years.

27. New York was 'born' on this day in 1664 when the English changed the name of the settlement from New Amsterdam. It is the birthday of Don Bradman, Australia's most famous cricketer of recent times.

28. Leo Tolstoy, one of Russia's greatest writers, was born on this day in 1828. His most famous books are *War and Peace* and *Anna Karenina*.

29. The anniversary of the birth of Jean Ingres, one of France's greatest portrait painters. Today is also the birthday of England's popular motor racing hero James Hunt.

30. Ernest Rutherford, the scientist who was the first to make successful experiments on splitting the atom, and thus paved the way for the study of nuclear physics, was born on this day in 1871. It is also the anniversary of the birth of Mary Wollstone-craft Shelley, the author of the original story of *Frankenstein*. She got the idea for the tale about a man-made man from a dream.

31. The birthday of Sir Bernard Lovell, the astronomer. This is the feast day of St Aidan, who began one of the first schools in England for boys on the island of Lindisfarne, off the Northumberland coast, and now called Holy Island. The ruined site of the monastery where the boys were taught more than thirteen centuries ago can still be seen.

August

Birthday Dates	16
1	17
2	18
3	19
4	20
5	21
6	22
7	23
8	24
9	25
10	26
11	27
12	28
13	29
14	30
15	31

September

The month of chilly, misty mornings brings more signs of autumn everywhere. The hours of daylight become four or five minutes shorter each day, and the tilt of the earth means that even when the sun shines brightly the day is no longer very warm. In the country the harvesting of grain and fruit is almost over, and many fields are now bare and brown as the ploughmen prepare them for yet another year ahead.

Rather strangely many birds begin to sing again, and there is much activity as they eat voraciously to store up energy against the lean times of winter. Some birds are preparing to leave for warmer lands – the blackcap, sandpiper, martin and swallow. And the first of our winter birds begin to arrive – the fieldfare, redwing and woodcock among them.

September has a number of modern festivals. Australia was proclaimed a Commonwealth on September 17, 1900, and September 15 is Battle of Britain Day, in commemoration of the victory in the summer of 1940 by the R.A.F. over the German Luftwaffe.

In that wartime year September brought day after day of fine weather, and this often happens in this autumnal month. The sign of a long spell of fine weather is said to be the way cattle and sheep graze with their heads facing towards the wind.

Not until almost the end of the month is there an important and ancient festival – Michaelmas, on September 29, in honour of the Archangel Michael. He is specially honoured by soldiers as their protector and by sick people for whom he is a special guardian.

Michaelmas used to be a sort of working holiday. By that time the yield of the harvest was known and people could estimate how much food they had for themselves and their farm animals to take them through the winter, while merchants had collected plenty of goods to sell.

As a result there were great Michaelmas fairs and sales of food and animals in every market town, the serious activities of buying and selling during the day ending with singing and dancing in the evening.

Employers went around engaging new workers, and in many places there were hiring markets where jobs for a year ahead were offered and accepted. Boys were engaged as apprentices to skilled trades. 'I'm a Michaelmas apprentice' was the proud boast of many a new teenager.

The traditional food to serve when the busy hours of buying and selling were over was a goose. The modern idea that the wishbone from roast poultry brings luck to anyone who gets it in a portion of meat originated with the Michaelmas goose. The old belief was that it meant luck in love if it did not easily break, and luck in material prosperity if it broke at the first tug.

September

1. Two saints have their festival today. St Fiacre became well known for the fine flowers and vegetables he grew around his hermitage near Meaux in France, with the result that he became the patron saint of gardeners. St Giles, who protected his pet deer with his own body when hunters shot an arrow and was himself wounded by it, is the patron saint of cripples and beggars. This is a day marking the birthday of two Canadian provinces, Alberta and Saskatchewan, founded in 1905.

2. The anniversary of the day in 1666 that the Great Fire of

London broke out, starting in a bakery in Pudding Lane. It burned for four days and nights. It is the birthday of Jimmy Connors, American tennis champion.

3. Britain declared war on Germany in 1939.

4. This is Labor Day in the U.S.A. when many workpeople have a holiday. It is the feast day of St Marinus, a saint with a tiny republic named after him – San Marino in Italy. He was a stone-mason and is locally the patron saint of all who work with stones and rocks.

5. The birth date of John Wisden in 1826. He was a sports outfitter who began keeping notes about cricket matches, and eventually published his records for the year 1864. Since then his Almanack has been published every year and is the 'bible' of cricket.

6. The anniversary of a sad day when, in 1939, there could be no further new and wonderful drawings of elves, gnomes and fairies for children's books, for Arthur Rackham, the best known of all illustrators of stories like *Rip Van Winkle*, *Peter Pan*, and Hans Andersen's tales, died. It is the feast day of St Magnus, the protector of farmers. It was said that he had a walking stick which protected crops from pests and harmful insects.

7. Queen Elizabeth I was born on this day in 1533.

8. The birthday of two popular entertainers: Harry Secombe, one of the original Goons and a talented singer; and Jimmie Rodgers, the first of the great country-style singers.

9. The 'Demon Bowler', Frederick Robert Spofforth, was born on this day in 1853. This famous Australian cricketer's feat in taking fourteen wickets for ninety runs in an Australia v. England match at the Oval in 1882 led to the burning of a cricket stump, its ashes becoming a symbol of Test matches between the two countries. John Curry, holder of World, European and Olympic titles for ice skating, was also born on this day.

10. The feast day of St Finnian of Moville. In Ulster where he was born and lived, he is regarded as the patron saint of booksellers and book lovers.

11. The Battle of Malplaquet, a great victory for the English under the Duke of Marlborough against the French, took place on this day in 1709. Today is the birthday of world champion racing motor cyclist Barry Sheene.

12. The birthday of Roald Dahl, author of many children's stories. It is the feast day of St Guy of Anderlecht, whose life was associated with horses. In many towns and villages in France and Belgium horse riders and cab drivers used to hold processions on September 12 in the saint's honour.

13. The anniversary of a battle in 1759 which decided the future of Canada, when English troops under General Wolfe defeated the French under General Montcalm on the Heights of Abraham at Quebec, and Canada became a British possession. It is the birthday of J. B. Priestley, noted author.

14. Peter Scott, artist and authority on wild birds, has his birthday today. He is the son of Robert Scott, the explorer. In Austria farmers claim that they can always rely on a period of fine weather from sunset on this day. The legend is that St Notburga, then a peasant girl, refused to work on a Sunday as the farmer had told her to do because the weather might change.

'Let this decide,' said Notburga, who threw her sickle into the air. It soared upwards and stayed motionless high in the sky like a crescent moon in a clear sky, a certain indication of prolonged fine weather.

15. This is Battle of Britain day, in honour of the fighter pilots of the R.A.F. who on this day in 1940 fought their greatest battle against the German Luftwaffe and saved Britain from invasion. James Fenimore Cooper, the first American author to write novels about Red Indians and the Wild West, was born on this day in 1789. Another famous novelist with this birth date was Agatha Christie, the most successful British writer of detective stories.

16. The birthday of Louis XIV, King of France, whose reign lasted for seventy-two years. The palace he built at Versailles is one of the most magnificent buildings in Europe.

17. On this day in 1900 Australia was proclaimed a Commonwealth. Birthdays: Stirling Moss, motor racing champion, and Hank Williams, the rock and western singer.

18. Dr Johnson, poet, author, and critic, was born on this day in 1709. He compiled the first good dictionary which, with the help of six assistants, took him eight years. It is the birthday of Peter Sellers, the actor famous for his humorous roles.

19. The anniversary of a historic battle in 1356 at Poitiers in France when the Black Prince led his troops to a great victory over the French. It is the birthday of Greta Garbo, regarded by many people as the greatest film star of all time.

20. The birthday of Sophia Loren, Italy's best known film star.

21. H. G. Wells, author of such famous stories as *The Invisible Man*, *The Time Machine*, and *The War of the Worlds*, was born on this day in 1866.

22. Michael Faraday was born this day in 1791. He became one of the most famous scientists of his time and invented the electric motor and the dynamo. He was largely self-taught; as an errrand boy for a bookseller at the age of twelve he borrowed and read every book in the shop he could find time to read. Faraday started the Christmas Lectures at the Royal Institution, which have been held ever since for boys and girls.

23. The birthday of Ray Charles, known as 'the father of soul music'. He went blind at the age of six and had lost both parents by the time he was fifteen. Many of his records have topped the million sale mark.

24. The birthday of A. P. Herbert, author and playwright. His best known book is *The Water Gypsies*.

25. The feast day of one of Wales's best loved saints – Cadoc. Those born on his feast day in Brittany – where the saint also lived – are said to be blessed with the saint's proverbial wisdom.

On this day in 1513 man had a new glimpse of the vastness of his world, when Vasco de Balboa, a Portuguese explorer, first glimpsed the Pacific Ocean from Panama.

26. New Zealand became a Dominion on this day in 1907. Birthdays: George Gershwin, American composer, famous for *Rhapsody in Blue* and the opera *Porgy and Bess*; and Olivia Newton John, the only British singer ever to have been voted the best country and western singer by American fans.

27. The feast day of twin saints, the brothers Cosmos and Damian. They were famous doctors in the Middle East, but never charged their patients any fee. They are the patron saints of doctors.

28. The birthday of Prosper Mérimée, a French author of plays, novels and short stories, whose works are studied by every French pupil for their examinations in literature – and often in British schools for A-levels in the French language.

29. Michaelmas, marking the traditional last day for getting in the harvest. This is the feast day of the archangel Michael, regarded as the protector of soldiers in battle. It is the anniversary of the birth in 1758 of Horatio Nelson.

30. Botswana's day, in celebration of the country's independence granted in 1966.

September

Birthday Dates	16
1	17
2	18
3	19
4	20
5	21
6	22
7	23
8	24
9	25
10	26
11	27
12	28
13	29
14	30
15	

October

October has many old nicknames – the 'yellow month' because of the falling leaves, 'the wine month' in Europe as the last of the grapes are pressed, and 'the brewing month' in Britain because barley and malt are ready for making ale.

Although it marks the real autumn, and chilly days and cold nights are usual, October may bring a brief spell of fine and warm weather, starting around October 18, which is the feast day of St Luke. The saint presides over this nice break for getting outdoors – often luckily coinciding with half-term school holidays – and it has for long been known as St Luke's Summer. In the United States it is called the Indian Summer. The Red Indians regarded it as a special time for building their winter tepees and hunting the buffalo to obtain supplies of meat to help them through the approaching winter.

But the respite of mild weather is usually short. Tradition says that two saints, Simon and Jude, arrive on their feast day, October 28, with cold winds and rain to bring us winter.

All wild life heeds the warning of that day. The last of our summer visiting birds soon fly off. Geese and duck arrive in their thousands from the already cold areas of the North. Starlings, pigeons and finches abandon their solitary life and gather in flocks for mutual protection and food searching. And the robin brightens his red waistcoat, coming close to human habitation in the hope of food scraps.

Those insects which do not die fall into a state of suspended animation in dry crevices or below the surface of the soil. Frogs settle in the mud at the bottom of ponds, toads and snakes burrow into the earth. Furry animals grow thicker coats, and on some – blue hares, weasels, stoats – the summer fur falls out and is replaced by a dense white coat.

The last few hours of October are the most noteworthy, when Hallowe'en begins at twilight on the evening of October 31. In pagan times this day was the eve of the new year among the Celtic peoples of Western Europe, Wales and Ireland. The Celtic name for the day was Samain, and people used to light bonfires near the burial places of their ancestors and dance round the flames until only glowing embers were left. They then jumped over the ashes to ensure good fortune.

In later years the evening was called Apple and Candle Day. Children tried to bite apples floating in a bowl of water suspended from two crossed pieces of wood on which two candles were balanced.

If a boy or girl successfully lifted an apple with their teeth from the bowl or did so from the strings from the cross piece of wood without knocking over the candles, their future marriage partner would be reflected when they looked in a mirror. Or they could peel the apple, throw the peel in the air, and it would form the initial letter of the name of their future lover when it fell.

Any girl secretly in love with a boy could find out if her affection was returned when the Hallowe'en bonfire was just a pile of red hot ashes. She had to throw a hazel nut on the embers, whispering the boy's name and then saying aloud, 'If you love me pop and fly; if you don't, then smoulder and die.'

Hallowe'en was one of the few nights of the year when ghosts, witches and fairies came out and were visible to mortals. In Britain nowadays there are not many Hallowe'en celebrations, but in the United States children have a splendid time, going from house to house with lanterns, hollowed-out pumpkins with a lighted candle inside, and masks to make the wearers look like ghosts.

October

1. A nation's birthday celebrated by 800 million people – China Day. It is also the national day of Nigeria. Julie Andrews, star of *Mary Poppins* and many other films, has her birthday today.

2. The birthday of Graham Greene, author of a number of best-selling novels.

3. The feast day of the most popular saint of modern times: St Teresa. She only lived until she was twenty-four: a great church was built at Lisieux in Normandy, France, where she had lived and is now visited by tens of thousands of people from all over the world on her feast day.

4. The day the Space Age dawned, in 1957, when the Russians put the first artificial satellite, *Sputnik I*, into orbit.

5. The birthday of Donald Pleasance, the actor. It is the feast day of St Placid; in Sicily children born on this day are said to be given a serene and gentle temperament by the saint.

6. The anniversary of the birth of Quebec, founded as a colony in 1763. It is the birthday of Melvyn Bragg, the TV personality and author.

7. A historic anniversary for New Zealand. On this day in 1769 Captain James Cook landed on its coast and then sailed right round both North and South Islands. Ludmilla Tourischeva, Russian gymnast and winner of five gold medals in the 1975 World Cup gymnastics, has her birthday today.

8. The feast day of St Bridget; she lived in Sweden where she is one of the best known of the country's saints, and many Swedish girls are named after her. The nuns of her order, Brigittines, work for the sick and poor all over Europe; they have a nunnery, Syon House, in Devon.

9. Anniversary of the founding of Hobart, Tasmania, in 1804 as the country's capital. It is the birthday of John Lennon, the former Beatle.

10. The birth date of Giuseppi Verdi, composer of numerous operas, including *Rigoletto*, *La Traviata*, *Aida*, and several works based on Shakespeare's plays.

11. The birthday of Bobby Charlton, probably the most admired of modern soccer players; in his career he scored forty-nine goals for England.

12. The anniversary of one of the most momentous days in the history of man's exploration, when in 1492 Christopher Columbus stepped ashore on Watling's Island in the New World; he

did not realise he had discovered a new continent and thought he was on an island off the coast of Asia. On this day in 1875 New Zealand celebrated another step forward when the country was given a central government.

13. The feast day of an English king who became a saint: Edward the Confessor. On this day in 1814 the Cape of Good Hope became a British colony. The date marks the birthday of Mrs Margaret Thatcher, leader of the Conservative party; Wilfred Pickles, famous radio personality in the war and post-war period, and of Art Garfunkel, partner with Paul Simon in the famous pop music duo.

14. The history of England was changed on this day in 1066 when the invading Normans defeated the English at the Battle of Hastings. Birthdays: William Penn, founder of Pennsylvania; Dwight Eisenhower, World War Two general and U.S. President, and Cliff Richard, one of the first of the modern pop music singers.

15. The anniversary of the birth of P. G. Wodehouse, writer for more than seventy years of humorous books, notably those featuring Bertie Wooster and his valet Jeeves.

16. The first recognised flight by a powered aircraft in Britain took place at Farnborough in 1908. It is the birthday of Max Bygraves, the 'I wanna tell you a story' singer and entertainer.

17. The feast day of two little princes who were, according to legend, assassinated in their father's kingdom of Kent in the seventh century. They were Christians at a time when many of the English people were still pagans. The princes' names were Ethelbert and Ethelred, and until quite recently many Kentish boys were given one of these names.

18. The start of a brief warm period called St Luke's Summer; the saint whose feast day is celebrated today is the patron of artists and doctors. It is the anniversary of Alaska as part of the U.S.A.,

when in 1867 that country bought it from Russia. Birthday: Chuck Berry (real name Charles Edward Berry), the biggest star of rock 'n' roll music.

19. Anniversary of the birth of one of Australia's best-loved poets, Adam Lindsay Gordon; one of his verses is often quoted to Australian boys and girls as a motto for them to observe:

> Life is mostly froth and bubble,
> Two things stand like stone,
> Kindness in another's trouble,
> Courage in your own.

20. Anniversary of the birth of Sir Christopher Wren, architect of London's St Paul's cathedral and many other fine buildings and churches in the capital. This is the feast day of St Bertilla, patroness of nurses and hospital workers.

21. Trafalgar Day, commemorating the anniversary of the great victory in 1805 when Nelson defeated the French fleet and saved Britain from any risk of invasion. Birthdays: Samuel Coleridge, the author and poet who wrote *The Ancient Mariner*; Alfred Nobel, who left his fortune to finance the Nobel prizes; and Manfred Mann (real name Mike Lubowitz), pianist and leader of jazz bands.

22. Franz Liszt, composer, pianist and conductor, was born on this day in 1811.

23. The anniversary of the birth of Robert Bridges, the Poet Laureate in Queen Victoria's time.

24. Sarah Hale, an American author, was born on this day in 1788. She would hardly be known but for the fact that she wrote the nursery rhyme beginning 'Mary had a little lamb.' Today is the birthday of Jack Warner, famous as a music hall artist and star of the many TV and radio plays about the police.

25. Two famous battles took place on this day – Agincourt in 1415 and the Charge of the Light Brigade in 1854. Famous birthdays: Johann Strauss, the Viennese composer of waltzes; and Pablo Picasso, the greatest – and richest – painter of this century; when he was born his mother and nurse believed he was dead, but his uncle blew into his nostrils and he cried and began to breathe.

26. The national days of Austria and of Iran – the latter because it is the Shah's birthday.

27. Anniversary of the birth of Theodore Roosevelt in 1858. He became President of the U.S.A. and is also known as the man who inspired an American toy manufacturer to make a woolly animal to which he gave Roosevelt's nickname, 'Teddy'.

28. The feast day of two saints, St Simon and St Jude; the latter is regarded as a helper of those who are in desperate straits as regards health or money. St Simon is supposed to warn us that cold weather is near – 'winter approaching at a gentle trot'. On this day in 1929 a baby girl had a unique birthday. She was born to Mrs T. W. Evans in an aircraft flying over Miami – the first birth ever to take place in an airplane in flight.

29. The birthday of the Red Cross in 1863. This organisation for the relief of suffering was formed in Geneva by Jean Dunant, a Swiss banker, who was moved by the sufferings he saw among the wounded after the Battle of Solferino two years earlier.

30. The anniversary of the birth of two great writers: Richard Brinsley Sheridan, who wrote such plays as *The Rivals* and *The School for Scandal*; and Feodor Dostoievsky, the Russian author, considered one of the major novelists in the world's literature; he wrote *Crime and Punishment* and *The Brothers Karamazov*.

31. Hallowe'en, when ghosts are supposed to be abroad as soon as darkness falls. John Keats, who in his short life wrote the odes unexcelled by any other poet, was born on this day in 1795.

October

Birthday Dates	16
1	17
2	18
3	19
4	20
5	21
6	22
7	23
8	24
9	25
10	26
11	27
12	28
13	29
14	30
15	31

November

After all the spooky events of the last hours of October, dawn on November 1 brings more peaceful festivities. It is All Saints' Day or Hallowmas, in honour of the hundreds of saints of Christianity. It is a feast day which has been celebrated for more than a thousand years. Once it was a religious holiday when only essential work was done, and some countries still observe it as a national holiday.

November 5, Guy Fawkes Day, when there is a good excuse for bonfires and fireworks – though Fawkes's plot to blow up the Houses of Parliament with gunpowder was discovered before there could be any conflagration – is not just a British celebration. In many parts of Europe there are bonfires on this night, just as there were in ancient times when pagan people wanted to influence their gods to bring warmth back to the chilly earth while thanking them with sacrificial fires for the harvest of the autumn. Americans have adapted this celebration as their Thanksgiving Day, held on the fourth Thursday of the month. The Pilgrim Fathers held the first Thanksgiving Feast in 1621 after they had gathered in the first crops planted on their arrival in the New World from England.

In Scotland this final celebration of the year's harvest is held still later because their cool summers mean that crops are not ripe till fairly late. The Scots give thanks on the feast day of their patron, St Andrew.

Without these special days November would indeed be a

dreary month. 'No sun, no warmth, no flowers, no bird song, No-vember' is an old and all-too-true description. The worst period for cold, miserable weather is from November 6–13. More than a hundred years ago a Scotsman named Alexander Buchan carefully studied weather records and named this as one of the Buchan Cold Periods. Was he right in his forecast this year?

The countryside is silent. Birds no longer sing, and hibernating creatures such as hedgehogs settle down for their long winter sleep. But on commons you can still find a few sprays of yellow blossom on broom.

'When the gorse is out of bloom, kissing is out of fashion', warns an old adage. It's true enough, for there is no time of the year when these yellow flowers are entirely absent.

November

1. All Saints Day, once known as All Hallowmas, has been a festival for more than a thousand years, and earlier still among the pagan people of Wales and Ireland, for it was their new year's day. A child born on this day was always given the name of a saint to ensure a happy life.

2. Two anniversaries of the age of broadcast entertainment. On this day in 1920 the first sound broadcasting station went on the air from Pittsburg, and in 1936 the BBC started regular TV programmes from Alexandra Palace in North London.

3. The birthday of Viscount Linley (christened David Albert Charles), the son of Princess Margaret, born in 1961; and of Ludovic Kennedy, the TV interviewer and writer.

4. The feast day of St Charles Borromeo, an Italian who in the sixteenth century started the first known Sunday schools for children. In Italy boys and girls attending Sunday schools hold special celebrations on this day in the saint's honour.

5. Guy Fawkes Day provides a good reason for a special kind of party for anyone born on this day – with fireworks as well as presents.

6. The feast day of St Leonard, who lived in France. One day the king and queen of France were passing the cave where he lived as a hermit, when the queen realised the birth of her baby was near. St Leonard cared for her, and in gratitude the king gave him all the land he could ride round in a night on a donkey. St Leonard built a monastery on the land he thus obtained from the king.

7. One of the great railroads of the world, the Canadian Pacific, running for 2905 miles across Canada, was completed on this day in 1886. It is the birthday of Marie Curie, who with her husband studied the properties of radium and was the first woman to win the Nobel prize for chemistry.

8. An unusual feast day, honouring the Four Crowned Ones, with their names omitted. They were skilled stone carvers in Rome who died sooner than carve pagan statues. The day used to be observed as a holiday by quarrymen and sculptors, and the day is still specially honoured by men who are members of the Freemasons movement.

9. King Edward VII was born on this day in 1841. He was named Albert Edward, and was so popular as a prince and king that most people in Britain now have ancestors born up to a century ago with one or both of these names. It is the birthday of Katharine Hepburn, noted film actress.

10. The anniversary of a historical incident which is in all school books: the meeting of Stanley after his long search for Livingstone in Africa in 1871, with Stanley asking the famous question, 'Dr Livingstone, I presume?' It is also the anniversary of the birth of two men who in their different ways affected all our lives. Martin Luther, often called the founder of Protestant civilisation, was born in 1483; William Morris, whose artistry

changed for the better our furniture, textiles, household decorations, and books, was born in Walthamstow in 1834. It is also the birthday of Richard Burton, the actor.

11. Armistice Day in 1918, when the First World War came to an end. In some countries the day is celebrated on the nearest Sunday, but in others, such as France, it is still a public holiday. It is also appropriately St Martin's Day, in honour of the soldier who changed to a man of peace. To show he was no coward he offered to stand unarmed between opposing forces in a battle. He travelled all over Europe and Britain, and had the reputation of bringing fair weather with him, with the result that warm and sunny weather at this period is known at St Martin's summer: 'three days and a bit'.

12. The feast day of another Martin, St Martin the First, who was Pope in the seventh century. He suffered terribly in prison at the hands of the Emperor in Constantinople, and as a result he is regarded as the saint watching over people who are unjustly punished. Today is the birthday of Nadia Comaneci, Romanian gymnast champion at the Montreal Olympics.

13. The anniversary of the birth in 1850 of Robert Louis Stevenson, author of *Treasure Island* and *Kidnapped*.

14. Prince Charles was born on this day in 1948. Many men of the same age as the heir to the throne bear one of his names – Charles Philip Arthur George. When the Prince reached his twenty-

fifth birthday he had a special reason to celebrate, for it was the wedding day of his sister, Princess Anne. In 1922 the first BBC broadcast was made from a London station with the call sign 2LO. It is the anniversary of the birthdays of Auguste Rodin, the French sculptor, and Harold Larwood, famous cricketer.

15. The feast day of St Malo, a Welsh saint now better known in France, where he lived for most of his life on an island in the river beside which the Channel port of St Malo stands.

16. A feast day which explains why so many Scots girls are named Margaret. St Margaret was also a Scottish queen, the wife of Malcolm III. She was universally loved for her kindly nature, and organised help for orphans and poor people at a time when few people cared about them.

17. The anniversary of the birth of Bernard Montgomery, who as the General known to his troops as Monty achieved the famous victory of El Alamein and later led the British armies into the heart of Germany, accepting the surrender of the enemy forces on Luneberg Heath in May 1945.

18. The birthday of William S. Gilbert, who with Arthur Sullivan wrote the Gilbert and Sullivan operas, such as *The Pirates of Penzance* and *The Mikado*.

19. The birthday in 1600 of King Charles I whose reign ended so sadly in civil war and then his execution. People still put flowers on his statue at the top of Whitehall on this day. It is the feast day of St Elizabeth of Hungary, Germany's best loved saint – a princess who lived in dire poverty so she could give food and clothing to the needy.

20. On this day in 1947 Queen Elizabeth II, then Princess Elizabeth, married Prince Philip.

21. The anniversary of man's first successful journey by air in 1783. Two Frenchmen soared up in a balloon 300 feet over Paris and drifted gently in the wintry breeze for five miles,

landing safely in a field. Birthdays: Malcolm Williamson, the first Australian to be appointed Master of the Queen's Musick, and of twins: John and Roy Boulting, producers and directors of many British films.

22. George Eliot (real name Marian Evans) was born this day in 1819. She was one of the great authors of her time, and her novels, especially *Adam Bede*, *The Mill on the Floss*, and *Middlemarch*, are still popular. It is also the anniversary of the birth of Benjamin Britten, renowned composer, whose work *The Young Person's Guide to the Orchestra* has taught many thousands of children to understand and enjoy good music.

23. St Clement's Day. St Clement was the patron saint of sailors, and many churches in ports and harbours were built in his honour. The famous 'Oranges and Lemons' church in London of the nursery rhyme is known as St Clement's Danes because originally Danish sailors had lodging houses near it. For many years, and sometimes even now, children at school in the church's parish get an orange as a gift from the saint on this day.

24. The anniversary of the birth of Grace Darling. Her father was the lighthouse keeper on one of the Farne Islands off the Northumberland coast, and with him she rowed a boat through a terrible storm to rescue some shipwrecked sailors and became a national heroine as a result.

25. St Katherine's Day. Legend tells that she was a beautiful girl who lived in Egypt. She was tied to a wheel when she refused to worship idols, but it miraculously fell to pieces, with splinters flying everywhere, leaving Katherine quite unhurt. The catherine wheel whirling round with sparks flying off it in firework displays was originally a ritual in the saint's memory.

26. The anniversary of the birth of William Cowper, a poet who for all his life remembered how he had hated school and mentioned it in his verses. He wrote the well-known poem *John Gilpin*.

27. The birthday of Jimi Hendrix (real name James Marshall Hendrix) song writer, singer and guitarist.

28. William Blake, the poet, was born on this day in 1757. Almost every schoolboy and schoolgirl reads and learns his poem beginning:

> Tiger! Tiger! burning bright,
> In the forest of the night.

29. The anniversary of the birthday of Louisa May Alcott, the American author who wrote *Little Women*.

30. St Andrew's Day. St Andrew is the patron saint of Scotland and his emblem of a cross saltire (X) appears in the Union Jack. One occasion when Scots specially celebrated the day was in 1872 when the first international football match took place: Scotland versus England. Jonathan Swift, who wrote *Gulliver's Travels*, was born on this day in 1667; Samuel Clemens, better known as Mark Twain, author of *Tom Sawyer* and other stories about boys in America, was born on this day in 1835. But the great anniversary is the birth of Winston Churchill at Blenheim Palace, Oxfordshire, in 1874. He arrived in this world earlier than expected: his birthday should have been in January or early February – his premature birth helping to confirm that 'seven month' babies are clever, energetic, and assured of a long life.

November

Birthday Dates	16
1	17
2	18
3	19
4	20
5	21
6	22
7	23
8	24
9	25
10	26
11	27
12	28
13	29
14	30
15	

December

The Christmas festivities used to begin earlier than they do to-day, if we don't count the shops and stores which decorate their windows and display festive gifts weeks before the great day. The old custom was to regard December 6 as the beginning of 'the long Christmas', lasting until the candles were snuffed out at Candlemas on February 2.

December 6 is the feast of St Nicholas, the patron of children and the origin of Santa Claus, which is a name derived from Dutch words for the saint – Sinte Klaas. He is supposed to have rescued three little girls from hunger and poverty by giving each of them a bag of gold. In parts of Eastern Europe, where St Nicholas lived in the fourth century, girls are still given some present coloured yellow, often a saffron cake, on December 6.

All through December people used to hang evergreen boughs of holly and ivy in the streets and outside the doors of their houses as a magical way of encouraging summer greenery to return, and to drive off evil spirits wanting to shelter from the cold.

Before Christianity came to Britain December 24 was Mother's Day, when mothers were honoured with gifts, and their housework and cooking were undertaken by other members of the family.

No one ventured into the darkness on that night. It was a time when ghosts were abroad and farm animals talked. This strange occurrence would have been enticing except that to hear cows and sheep talking meant misfortune for the eaves-dropper and sometimes a prophecy of death. Even beehives had to be avoided, for the bees woke up on this night and hummed hymns and psalms, which no one should hear.

Christmas Day, easily the most joyous day of the year, has many strange traditions. At dawn cattle are said to kneel facing Bethlehem, the sun dances as it rises above the horizon, and the woodland spirits of good fortune seek the welcome shelter of pine branches when all the rest of the forest trees are bare and cold.

In many places a carefully stored bowl of corn from the autumn harvest used to be fed to the poultry and farm animals on Christmas morning to guard them against illness during the year ahead. The straw from that special crop of corn was spread below the cloth on the Christmas dinner table in honour of the animals which gave up their bedding for Christ's crib in the manger at Bethlehem. And on this day no one would go hunting wild animals for food. They too had a day of peace.

Most of the activities over Christmastide are believed to affect the rest of the year. Eating twelve mince pies in twelve different houses ensures twelve happy months ahead, and if the sun manages to shine even for a few minutes on Christmas Day then the weather will bring plentiful crops right through the coming year.

December

1. There's an old tradition that anyone born on this day is given three gifts: a generous nature, the desire to travel, and wisdom. Queen Alexandra, great-great-grandmother of Elizabeth II, was born on this day. Another December 1 baby: Gilbert O'Sullivan, born in 1946 in Eire and christened Raymond. He began his pop music career when in his teens.

2. Boys born in France on this day are often given the name Napoleon, for it is the anniversary of their national hero's greatest victory over the Russians and Austrians at Austerlitz in 1805. A sad memory is that on this day Robert Louis Stevenson, author of *Treasure Island* and *Kidnapped*, died in Samoa.

3. Joseph Conrad, writer of adventure and sea stories, was born on December 3; so was Rowland Hill, originator of the Penny Post, with a coloured piece of paper affixed to a letter as the fee no matter how far in the country its destination.

4. The birthdate of Samuel Butler, who wrote a famous story of a perfect country called *Erewhon* (an anagram of nowhere); of Maria Callas, one of this century's greatest operatic singers; and of Michael Bates, often seen in TV plays and sometimes disguised as an Indian – he grew up in that country and speaks the language fluently.

5. On this day in 1901 Walt Disney was born. In 1923 he created his cartoon character Mickey Mouse, soon adding Minnie Mouse, Pluto the Dog, and Donald Duck. His first full length cartoon film, *Snow White and the Seven Dwarfs*, involving scores of artists and hundreds of thousands of drawings, was finished in 1937, and was followed by all the cartoon and other films which have delighted children the world over ever since.

6. The feast of St Nicholas, the patron saint of children. Children born on this day used to get an extra gift which parents told them came from their saint. It is the birthday of a new nation: the Irish Free State came into being when a treaty was signed on this day in 1921. Pop music enthusiasts remember this day as the anniversary of the biggest free festival ever, when in 1969 in a speedway stadium in California the Rolling Stones gave a concert for 400,000 fans.

7. An ominous day in the history of the United States when, in 1941, Pearl Harbour was attacked without warning by the Japanese and many US naval ships were sunk. A much happier

event has a musical flavour: this is the birthday of Edmundo Ros, leader of a popular band playing South American music, and of Harry Chapin, one of America's pop singers of narrative numbers, such as *Cats in the Cradle* and *Heads and Tales*.

8. In Finland there are concerts and special programmes on radio and TV to mark the anniversary of the birth of the country's greatest composer, Sibelius. It is also the birthday of Gregg Allman, who formed the Allman Brothers Band, America's number one country style group. It's not surprising that Gregg was born in Nashville, Tennessee, traditional home of this kind of folk music.

9. The anniversaries of two people who probably affect your schooldays one way or another. The poet John Milton, whose works are frequently the subject of O- and A-level examinations, was born on this day in 1608; and Lord Butler, who carried through an Act in 1944 which created the system of state education for all children in our schools and colleges today.

10. A great date for grouse and other game birds, for the season when they can be hunted and shot ends today. It is also the anniversary of a date when the world grew smaller: in 1919 two Australian brothers, Ross and Keith Smith, flew from Britain to Australia in 135 hours, the first airmen ever to have done so.

11. The birthday of Cliff Michelmore, the TV personality; Hector Berlioz, famous French composer; and Alexander Solzhenitsyn, best known of living Russian authors.

12. Kenya Day, when that country became an independent republic of the British Commonwealth in 1963. Frank Sinatra

was born on this day and has been a top singer for more than forty years. The best birthday gift he probably ever had was the news that his record *My Way* had remained in the Top Twenty Charts for 120 weeks in 1970–72.

13. If it is a windy day don't be surprised. There are often gales at this time, and on December 13, 1967, the wind blew at 408 miles per hour high above the Outer Hebrides. The day has two patron saints, Lucy and Odilia, and both are considered to protect the eyes. In Alsace, where St Odilia lived in the eighth century, people make a pilgrimage on this festival to her shrine in the Vosges mountains.

14. King George VI, father of our Queen, was born on this day in 1895. It was also a historic day for exploration when, in 1911, Roald Amundsen, a Norwegian, reached the South Pole.

15. The man who was said to have played his fiddle while the city he ruled was burning, the Roman Emperor Nero, was born on this day in AD 37. A modern anniversary is that of Harold Abrahams, one-time Olympic gold medallist and the organiser of national facilities for sports and athletics for young people.

16. Plenty of parties to celebrate birthdays but never a party like that which took place in Boston, America, on this day in 1773. It was a tea party with a difference: tea chests were thrown into the water as a protest against the British government's attempt to enforce the importation of tea by colonists in America. Fifty men, disguised as Red Indians, climbed aboard the ships and overboard went 342 chests of tea. On this historic day a small boy named Ludwig von Beethoven had his third birthday, and two years later Jane Austen, the author of *Pride and Prejudice*, was born. Two modern people with this birthdate were Jack Hobbs, a great cricketer, and Noel Coward, the playwright.

17. In twelve seconds history was made on this day in 1903 when Orville Wright made the first power-driven flight in an aircraft. He managed to lift the machine twelve feet above the

head of his brother, Wilbur, and the speed of the aircraft was about the same as a running man. The day is the anniversary of the birth of Humphry Davy, the Cornishman who was one of the greatest scientists of his age, discovering sodium and potassium, and inventing the miner's safety lamp.

18. The birthday of a schoolmaster turned actor, poet and playwright – Christopher Fry, whose best known play is *The Lady's Not for Burning*. Keith Richard of the Rolling Stones was born this day in 1943; he first met Mick Jagger when both were in primary school.

19. Eamonn Andrews, TV commentator and compère of the *This is Your Life* programme has his birthday today. So does Sir Ralph Richardson, stage and film actor, famous for his portrayal of Falstaff in Shakespeare's plays.

20. This day used to be known as St Thomas's Eve and was widely regarded as a day when young people fell in love for the first time. A girl would stick nine pins or slivers of wood into an onion or apple, at the same time saying, 'Dear St Thomas, do me right; send me a vision of my true love tonight.' She then went to bed and with luck would have a dream in which she would see the man who wanted to marry her.

21. Although the eve of the feast of St Thomas was a time for lovers, the actual saint's day – December 21 – was considered a fortunate one on which to be born, for it meant a life of honour and respect. The Saint is said to have travelled far into India after the Crucifixion preaching Christianity, and in India Christians in Kerala still hold special celebrations on this day. It is the birthday of Christine Evert, American tennis star.

22. The day of the winter solstice when the sun is farthest south from the equator. It is the feast day of St Frances, the first citizen of the United States to be named as a saint. She opened hospitals, schools and children's homes all over the American continent.

23. The anniversary of the birth of Samuel Smiles in 1812; his books such as *Self Help* and *Lives of the Engineers* were given to thousands of schoolboys as prizes for good work, and to inspire them to make a success of their careers in adult life.

24. The first advertised radio broadcast programme was transmitted on this day in 1906 from Brant Rock, Massachussetts, U.S.A., with a programme of music by Handel. It is the birthday of Colin Cowdrey, Kent cricketer who formerly captained the England team.

25. To be born on Christmas Day is supposed to be the most fortunate of all the days of the year – even if it means both Christmas and birthday gifts are combined. Often the special birthdate is indicated by giving Christmas babies such names as Noel, Noelle, Holly and – in some European countries – Jesus or Jesu. Princess Alexandra, married to Angus Ogilvie, was a Christmas Day baby, and so in 1642, was Isaac Newton, regarded as the greatest English scientist who ever lived, and known the world over as the man who formulated the laws of gravity.

26. In bygone times this was a day for more gifts, for employers gave their workmen and apprentices boxes of presents for good work during the year that was almost over. It is the feast day of St Stephen, the first man to die for his faith in Christ's teaching.

27. This is the feast day of St John, and because Jesus named him and his brother James the 'sons of thunder', people believe that it is always possible to hear a rumble of thunder on this day.

28. The birthday of the cinema; the first public one was opened in Paris in 1895, in a room with seats for thirty-three people. They saw ten films, each lasting two or three minutes. This is Holy Innocents Day, in memory of the small children killed on the orders of King Herod, and for many centuries children all over Europe went to church on this day and sang special hymns; they still do so in the church of the Nativity in Bethlehem.

29. Two notable men were born on this day – William Gladstone, the nineteenth-century statesman, and Charles Macintosh, who was the principal inventor of waterproof clothing and the pneumatic tyre; the latter he made so that his little son, who was delicate, could ride a tricycle without being badly shaken as he pedalled around the cobbled streets of Dublin. December 29 is held in honour of St Thomas, but hardly a feast day, for it commemorates the terrible event when Thomas à Becket was murdered in Canterbury Cathedral in 1170.

30. A famous writer to have his birthdate today was Rudyard Kipling, author of *The Jungle Book* and the school story *Stalky and Co*, as well as scores of short stories.

31. The last day of the year used to bring a brief break in the seasonal festivities, with preparations of food and drink in readiness for the renewed celebrations to greet the New Year at midnight. It is the anniversary of the first supersonic flight by a passenger aircraft, the Russian TU144, in 1968. Peter May, the cricketer, was born on this date; so was John Denver, the folk singer and composer.

December

Birthday Dates	16
1	17
2	18
3	19
4	20
5	21
6	22
7	23
8	24
9	25
10	26
11	27
12	28
13	29
14	30
15	31

Birthday Tricks and Stunts

You probably know the age of most of your friends, so this stunt is best played with an adult who is quite certain you don't know how old he is.

Tell him to think of his age, but not to tell you. Next ask him to multiply his age by 3, then to add 6, and finally to divide that sum by 3. Ask for that figure. You subtract 2 from it, and the result is the person's age.

For example, perhaps you are playing this stunt on an uncle who is 34. On your instructions he multiplies this age by 3, getting 102. To this he adds 6 = 108. He divides by 3, which gives a figure of 36. You subtract 2, announcing correctly that your uncle's age is 34.

* * *

This stunt to find out someone's age is more complicated, and your subject should have pencil and paper so he can work out the sums.

Tell him that you will not only give his age but also the month in which he was born if he will write down certain information when you order it – without letting you know, of course.

First, ask him to write down the number of his birthday month – 1 for January, 2 for February, and so on to 12 for December. You tell him to multiply this figure by 2. Now he is ordered to add 5, and then multiply this figure by 50. (Give him a moment or two to allow him to make certain he has got the correct answer). To this figure he must add his age on his last birthday. Next you tell him to subtract the number of days in a year – 365 – which will probably take him a little time. Finally he is asked to add 115, and to give you the resulting number.

If there are two figures in it the first will be the birth month and the second the age; with three figures the first will be the month and the last two the age; four figures, and the first two will be the month and the last two the age.

Here are two examples:

Birth month January	1	Birth month December	12
Multiply by 2	2		24
Add 5	7		29
Multiply by 50	350		1450
Add age (say 9)	359	(Age say 15)	1465
Subtract 365	minus 6		1100
Add 115	109		1215
109 = Month 1 (January)		1215 = Month 12 (December)	
Age 9		Age 15	

*   *   *

Now for a simpler 'find your age' stunt. Tell your subject to multiply his age by 3, add 1, multiply by 3 again, add his age and give you the answer. Ignore the last figure (the unit); the other figure or figures give the age. Here are two examples:

Age		5		13
Multiply by 3		15		39
Add 1		16		40
Multiply by 3		48		120
Add age	(5)	53	(13)	133
Ignore last figure.				
Age		5		13

*   *   *

And one more easy age-finding trick. Tell your subject to

think of his age last birthday, multiply by 2, add 1. Then multiply by 5 and add 5, finally multiply by 10. Ask your subject for the result. You can then tell him his age by subtracting 100 and ignoring the last two figures. Examples:

Age	9	14
Multiply by 2	18	28
Add 1	19	29
Multiply by 5	95	145
Add 5	100	150
Multiply by 10	1000	1500
Subtract 100 and ignore last two figures	900	1400
Age	9	14

* * *

This is a more impressive stunt, as you can discover both your subject's age and any number (below 100) he also chooses. Tell him to think of his age, multiply it by 2, add 5, and multiply by 50. From this total he must subtract the number of days in the year – 365. Lastly he adds any number below 100 he likes to think of, and give you the result. To this you add 115 without telling your subject. The first two figures give your subject's age and the last two the number he chose.

Examples:

Age	8	15
Multiply by 2	16	30
Add 5	21	35
Multiply by 50	1050	1750
Subtract 365	685	1385
Add a number under 100 (say 47)	732	(say 9) 1394
Add 115	847	1509
	Age is 8 and number thought of 47	Age is 15 and number thought of 9

What day was it?

Perhaps you or your friends do not know on what day you were born, although, of course, you know the date. Or when you read of the date of some great event you would like to know what day it was. You can work this out, and the arithmetic is not too difficult if you tackle it slowly and check each item. Or maybe you have a calculator?

You must add up the following numbers:

1. The year (1899, 1978, and so on).
2. The number obtained by dividing the year's number by 4. You ignore any fractions or decimals, so if you took the year 1899, that divided by 4 is $474\frac{3}{4}$ or 474·75; you just put 474 on your list.
3. Multiply the number of completed centuries before your year by 6. This is the 20th century, so 19 have been completed.
4. Divide the number of completed centuries by 4, again ignoring fractions or decimals. Thus $19 \div 4 = 4\frac{3}{4}$ or 4·75; you put 4 on your list.
5. The key number of the month from Table A (see page 143).
6. The number of the day of the month of your birthday or the event which interests you.
7. Add these six figures up and divide by 7, making a note of the remainder.
8. The figure for the remainder is then looked up in Table B (see page 143), which will give you the name of the day.

You can use this system for any date as far back as 1753. Before then, as explained on pages 16 and 17, we used a different calendar and the sum will not work out.

Test this idea by using today's date or your own birthdate if your parents are really sure of the name of the day on which you were born. They are not always absolutely certain!

Leap years occur when the year is exactly divisible by 4, except for 1900 and – in the future – 2100, 2200 and 2300.

Here are two examples to help you understand what you have to do. September 3, 1939, was the day the Second World War broke out, and all your history books will have told you that it was a Sunday. As Christmas Day in 1977 also falls on a Sunday, let us take Boxing Day, Monday December 26, as the other example:

	September 3, 1939	December 26, 1977
The year's number	1939	1977
Divide the year by 4 and ignore fractions	484	494
Completed centuries multiplied by 6 – 19 × 6	114	114
Completed centuries divided by 4, and ignore fractions – 19 ÷ 4	4	4
The key number of the month from Table A	5	5
The number of the day	3	26
Total	2549	2620
Divide by 7	364 (remainder 1)	374 (remainder 2)
Look up remainder in Table B	1 = Sunday	2 = Monday

More Beaver Books

We hope you have enjoyed this Beaver Book. Here are some of the other titles:

The Beaver Book of Games   A Beaver original. George and Cornelia Kay describe dozens of games to play indoors and outdoors, including all the old favourites plus lots of new ones. Illustrated by Robin Anderson

Be Kind to Mum and Dad   A Beaver original. Gyles Brandreth's fun-filled book of ideas for being kind to Mum and Dad, from helping in the house to jokes and riddles to cheer them up, illustrated by Mik Brown and Wendy Lewis

Desperate Journey   Martluk the Eskimo boy finds that rescue is dependent on him when the plane in which he is travelling with three middle-aged Americans crashes in the frozen forests of Arctic Canada. A gripping novel by the explorer J. M. Scott

All Your Own   A Beaver original. Hundreds of ideas for transforming all – or part – of an ordinary bedroom into an exciting place to suit all your needs. Written by Elizabeth Gundrey and illustrated by Virginia Smith

The Beaver Book of Extra Money   A Beaver original. Dozens of ideas for earning extra money in your spare time, from exercising dogs to helping out at children's parties. Humorous illustrations by Mik Brown accompany Merry Archard's lively text for readers of ten upwards

Covens and Cauldrons   An anthology of stories, folk tales, poems and legends about witches, edited by Jacynth Hope-Simpson and strikingly illustrated by Krystyna Turska

New Beavers are published every month and if you would like the *Beaver Bulletin* – which gives all the details – please send a large stamped addressed envelope to:

Beaver Bulletin
The Hamlyn Group
Astronaut House
Feltham
Middlesex TW14 9AR

314243

Table A

January 0
January (leap year) 6
February 3
February (leap year) 2
March 3
April 6
May 1
June 4
July 6
August 2
September 5
October 0
November 3
December 5

Table B

Remainder 1 Sunday
2 Monday
3 Tuesday
4 Wednesday
5 Thursday
6 Friday
0 Saturday